LUCY CALKINS AND AMANDA HARTMAN

Authors as Mentors

DEDICATION

To Ruth Sweeny, who understands that school leadership, policy, and teaching can combine to give all children and teachers a voice.

FirstHand
An imprint of Heinemann
A division of Reed Elsevier Inc.
361 Hanover Street
Portsmouth, NH 03801-3912
www.heinemann.com

Offices and agents throughout the world

Copyright © 2003 by Lucy Calkins and Amanda Hartman

Photography: Peter Cunningham

The authors and publisher wish to thank those who have generously given permission to reprint borrowed material:

Excerpt from *The Other Way to Listen* by Byrd Baylor. Text Copyright © 1978 by Byrd Baylor. Reprinted with the permission of Atheneum Books for Young Readers, an imprint of Simon & Schuster Children's Publishing Division.

Text and cover from *Joshua's Night Whispers* by Angela Johnson, illustrated by Rhonda Mitchell. Published by Orchard Books, an imprint of Scholastic Inc. Text Copyright © 1993 by Angela Johnson. Illustration Copyright © 1993 by Rhonda Mitchell. Reprinted by permission.

Continued on page 132.

Library of Congress Cataloging-in-Publication Data

Calkins, Lucy McCormick.
   Authors as mentors / Lucy Calkins and Amanda Hartman.
   p. cm. — (Units of study for primary writing ; 5)
   ISBN 0-325-00529-X (pbk. : alk. paper)
   1. English language-Composition and exercises-Study and teaching (Primary)—United States. 2. Authors-Study and teaching (Primary)—United States. 3. Curriculum planning-United States. I. Hartman, Amanda. II. Title.
   LB1529.U5C35 2003   2003019534
   372.62'3--dc22

Printed in the United States of America on acid-free paper

07   06   05   ML   4   5

SERIES COMPONENTS

▶ **The Nuts and Bolts of Teaching Writing** provides a comprehensive overview of the processes and structures of the primary writing workshop.

▶ You'll use **The Conferring Handbook** as you work with individual students to identify and address specific writing issues.

▶ The seven **Units of Study**, each covering approximately four weeks of instruction, give you the strategies, lesson plans, and tools you'll need to teach writing to your students in powerful, lasting ways. Presented sequentially, the Units take your children from oral and pictorial story telling, through emergent and into fluent writing.

▶ To support your writing program, the **Resources for Primary Writers CD-ROM** provides video and print resources. You'll find clips of the authors teaching some of the lessons, booklists, supplementary material, **reproducibles** and **overheads**.

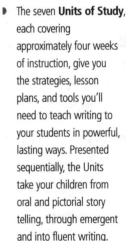

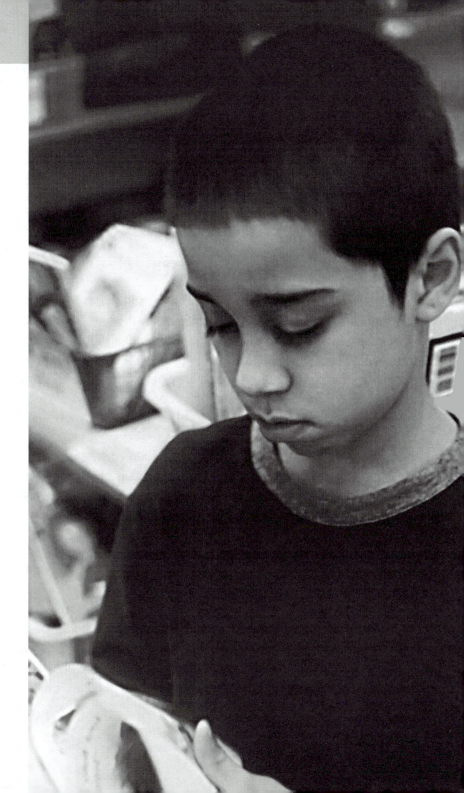

AUTHORS AS MENTORS

Eleanor Roosevelt, perhaps the most admired person in the world during her time, embodied the message that an ordinary person—she was plain in appearance, plain in dress, and plain in speech—can make an extraordinary difference. "I do believe," she said more than once, "that a few people who want to understand, to help, and to do the right thing, for the greater number of people instead of for the few, can help." In a similar way, Martin Luther King Jr., coming from the southern black community, embodied his story by rising above the pain and suffering he encountered in order to take up a ministry of reconciliation and invite others into it. "I have a dream that one day on the red hills of Georgia the sons of former slaves and the sons of former slave owners will be able to sit down together at a table of brotherhood. . . . I have a dream that my four children will one day live in a nation where they will not be judged by the color of their skin but by the content of their character," he said. He was an effective leader because he not only told but also embodied that story.

Why This Unit?

In the same way that Eleanor Roosevelt and Martin Luther King Jr. had a story to tell and to embody, teachers of writing do as well. The story is this: Ordinary people who live ordinary lives—people like you and me— can write like writers. We can write stories, poems, and books like those of the authors we admire. In a writing workshop, this is the essential message. We launch the writing workshop by saying, "We'll gather here in this library corner because here we are wrapped in books. Every one of these books was written by an author and this year, you will all be authors too."

It makes absolute sense, then, that for at least one month during the school year, our instructional focus must be on helping children learn to write by apprenticing themselves to authors they admire. A unit of study devoted to the study of an author will not be a revolutionary, new idea. In a sense, every unit incorporates studies of authors and their texts. For example, when our unit focuses on personal narrative writing, children study an author or two who has written personal narratives. However, devoting a month to a study of one or more authors creates an opportunity to approach the ongoing, continuing work of learning to write with a new angle.

I learned to write by apprenticing myself to Pulitzer prize-winning writer, Donald Murray. For me, this author study began when I read Murray's ground-breaking book, *A Writer Teaches Writing*. I was a recent college graduate, living alone with my dog in an ocean-side village, teaching, and trying to find my place in the world. Evenings, I'd often walk by the sea, yearning to find my path through life. Then, one day I read *A Writer Teaches Writing*, and the book seemed to lay out a path for me—just as the sun does glistening on the ocean—and my life has never been the same. I reread that book over and over until it became part of me, and with each successive reading it became more a part of me. The book guided my actions as a writer and a teacher. Through the pages of his book, Murray became my tutor, my coach, my North Star.

Of course, Murray's book came into my life when I was at the brink of adulthood, yearning for a mission, and his was not only beautiful literature, it was also a how-to book of the grandest nature. The authors our children read and love may not look our children in the eyes and speak to them quite so directly. But on the other hand, five- and six-year-old children are on the brink of their lives; they are standing at the threshold of the world of written language and they are asking, "Who am I?" and "How do I fit into this world?"

What a beautiful thing it is for us to answer, "You are the authors of your own life stories."

About the Unit

Just as Amanda Hartman (a colleague of mine at the Teachers College Reading and Writing Project) and I began this work with author studies, Patricia Polacco spoke to our community. Her speech made us long to dazzle our children with lush stories of Polacco's childhood. We were enthralled with all the goodies we could bring into classrooms—the reams of pages describing Patricia's writing style, her lush and engaging books, and the audio and videotapes about her. But, in the end, we came to the conclusion that she and the other authors for which such materials were readily available were more suitable as subjects for upper-elementary-level author studies. This doesn't mean that kindergarten and first grade children can't listen to and love Patricia Polacco's books or profit from a study of her stories. But when an author study is central to a writing workshop, our message must be, "You, too, can write like this." We doubted kindergarteners and first graders could even dream their writing might resemble the writing of Patricia Polacco or Eve Bunting or any number of other wonderful authors.

Our worry was that if our children studied an author whose writing was well beyond anything they could write, children might collect facts about an author rather than emulate the writer's style and process. Steven Kellogg has Great Danes, Jean Craighead George's daughter is named Twig, James Howe kept a shoe box full of baseball cards under his bed when he was little. Mem Fox recently showed us a letter in which a six-year-old wrote, "You are a busy bee and I like your books what you wrote and how do you change your hair color?" Although no harm is done if children become intrigued by Mem Fox's hair color, Amanda and I wanted to be sure children learned matters of more consequence. We wanted an author study to be more than glorified trivial pursuit. We began to search, then, for an author who:

- Wrote at least one or two brief, chronological stories that resembled the focused personal narratives our children were writing
- Used writing techniques that we suspected our children might want to emulate
- Wrote in ways that could open our children's eyes to new possibilities

In the end, we found four authors we think are perfect for a K–2 author study (we know many others exist!):

Angela Johnson	*Joshua's Night Whispers*
	The Leaving Morning
	Do Like Kyla
Ezra Jack Keats	*The Snowy Day*
	Peter's Chair
	The Pet Show
Donald Crews	*Shortcut*
	Night at the Fair
	Bigmama's
Joanne Ryder	*My Father's Hands*
	The Snail's Spell
	One Small Fish

In the end, we decided to study Angela Johnson. The winner of the Coretta Scott King Award (on two occasions) and the ALA Notable Book Award, Angela Johnson is known for her chapter books (including *Toning the Sweep* and *Heaven*) her anthologies of poetry (including *The Other Side: Shorter Poems*), as well as for the picture books we planned to study.

Angela Johnson is an African American whose characters, like her, are African American. She writes of ordinary, everyday moments in families, of breakfasts and moving days and finding a nest of baby birds. Angela's best-known picture book may be *Do Like Kyla*, an endearing story of a younger sister who all day long, in one episode after another, emulates her big sister Kyla. But the book we fell in love with first was *Joshua's Night Whispers*, a very short book that tells the story of one small episode in young Joshua's night when he hears night whispers, follows them, and ends up in the safe arms of his father.

We didn't find books and videos describing Angela Johnson's life. We *did* learn that by the time she was seven years old, Angela Johnson knew that she wanted to be a writer. As a seven-year-old, she asked for a diary and she has never stopped writing since. She says that her writing today grows out of the fact that all her life she was surrounded by storytellers who instilled in her a rich sense of narrative.

The Course of This Unit of Study

We knew our message to children would be that they, like Angela Johnson, could write books that are beautiful and important. We knew, too, that we wanted children to learn that if they closely study what another author has done in order to write well, they can learn ways to make their own writing better.

Our plan was not to take children by the hand and show them one after another after another of the features we'd admired. Instead, we wanted to invite them to notice one thing that Angela Johnson does as a writer, to investigate whether she uses that technique in several places, to consider the effect this technique creates, and finally, to consider using the same technique in their own writing.

If *Authors as Mentors* had replaced (rather than followed) *Revision*, then children would have entered the unit having drafted, but not seriously revised, lots and lots of pieces. In such an instance, this study of Angela Johnson's craft could help them revise that writing they'd already done. After examining Angela Johnson's leads, for example, they could look back and revise their own leads. But for us, this author study *followed* a revision study and a two-week vacation. We knew, therefore, that we'd need to use this unit to resume the writing they'd done earlier in the year. Only after our children had been reminded of all they'd already learned and had re-committed themselves to this work, the study of Angela Johnson could help them learn new ways with words and new structures for organizing written texts. Our plan for this unit, then, was from the start a complex one.

Part One: Crafting as in Angela Johnson's Books

- We will tell children we've found an author who, like them, catches small moments on the page. We'll introduce them to Angela Johnson, and use her as a way to help children remember how to write small moments.
- We will spotlight Angela Johnson's keen observations, suggesting that writing well comes from an attentive, wide-awake life. To help children follow Angela's example, we'll equip them with a new tool, a 1½" x 3" Tiny Topics notepad, and we'll encourage children to carry the notepads through their lives, using them to catch and hold small details that can later evoke pieces such as those Angela writes.
- We'll tell children that it can help to study the work of a mentor author (in this case, Angela). "What do you notice that Angela has done in her writing? Why do you suppose she did that? Can you see that same technique used somewhere else in her writing?" Finally, the question is, "Can you try using that technique in your own writing?" In this way, we will help children learn that they can find their own writing lessons simply by studying texts they love.

- While helping students learn from an author, we'll help them understand that writers think not only about *what* they'll write but also about *how* they'll write. Writers see other writers using words in new ways, and they emulate techniques they admire.
- We help children notice Angela's ways with words. Whatever they notice, we plan to "get behind," helping them to see the significance of what she's done and to imagine the process she probably used to write this way. For example, if they notice that she writes with details, we can point out that writers often do some research in order to develop their ideas. We could then turn their observation about Angela's writing into a challenge to the children—in this case, into a challenge to observe and interview in order to gather more details for *their* stories.

Part Two: Working with a New Text Structure

- We'll help children notice that some of Angela Johnson's books are *not* focused stories but are instead list-like or Many Moments stories. *Do Like Kyla*, for example, is about how a little sister emulates her big sister in one event after another. The unit will become a study of Many Moments stories, and of the techniques authors use to write these well.
- Children begin to choose the structures for their writing and to write not only "small moment" narratives, but also "many moments" stories.

Parts Three and Four: Finding Writing Mentors in All Authors and Preparing for Publication

- Angela Johnson is just one author deserving of study. Children in the final days of the study learn that they can find their own authors to love and to emulate. Children study the new authors as they studied Angela, paying close attention to the structures of texts. The final message, then, is "Go to it!" resulting in a flurry of "I notice . . ." and "I'm going to try . . ." based on the students' observations of the writing of the new authors.

▶ Students will learn how authors can help them edit by teaching them about punctuation and other conventions, and how authors can help them prepare their writing for publication. We want our students to continue developing their identities as writers and to develop a broader repertoire of techniques and strategies that they carry with them through their lives; we want them to see the texts around them as a wealth of information about writing itself.

DISCOVERING SMALL MOMENTS, AS ANGELA MIGHT

GETTING READY

- *Joshua's Night Whispers*
- 2" x 1" tiny topics notepads, one for each child; buy spirals and cut them in thirds
- Construction paper that will fit neatly on the covers of the tiny topics notepads; write each child's name on a cover and paper clip these onto the spiral notebooks; have extras on hand
- Markers, pens, glue sticks, and other materials for decorating covers
- Paper for writing stories
- Letter to parents explaining the tiny topics notepads
- Books to read aloud preceding the minilesson: *The Other Way to Listen, The Wise Woman and Her Secret*
- Large, clear packing tape
- See CD-ROM for resources

THIS SESSION REPRESENTS THE OFFICIAL LAUNCH *for your author study. You will want to create ribbon-cutting excitement, and to make your children feel as if they are embarking on a whole new chapter in their writing lives. This will be a challenge because for the first few days of this study you'll ask children to resume writing Small Moment narratives as they have been.*

You'll want to consolidate the instructional ground you have already traveled so that this unit's new work can build on (rather than replace) previous instruction. Then your author study of Angela Johnson can help children make reading-writing connections.

When you introduce Angela Johnson, you'll stress not only that she's great, but that she writes just like your children do. You will want your children to adore Angela Johnson and also to identify with her. Then you'll encourage children to follow Angela Johnson's model by living wide-awake, attentive lives, and by recording tiny topics in their new, tiny notepads. This notepad will embody your new emphasis on living like real authors. By using Angela Johnson to encourage students to slow down and take note of their own lived lives, you'll help students write better.

In this session, then, you'll help students notice that Angela Johnson finds tiny moments to write about, and you'll help them try to do that themselves, as they have in the past.

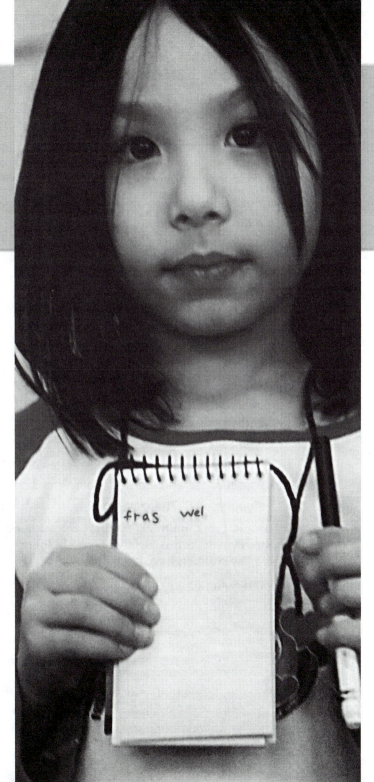

THE MINILESSON

Connection

Tell children that you recently found an author who writes just like them.

"I was in the town library this weekend and I found this book," Amanda held up *Joshua's Night Whispers*. "I read it, and I thought, 'This is *just like* the books you kids write!' Let me read it to you." Amanda read the forty-three-word book lovingly.

> In the nighttime the wind brings night whispers, so I follow them . . . past my toybox . . . and out my door . . . then down the hall. Night whispers all around. At last Daddy's holding me warm and safe and we listen together to the night whispers.

"When I find a book that's a lot like books I'm trying to write, I sometimes say—'Wait a minute. Maybe this author could be a teacher, a mentor for me. I could see *how* she does this kind of writing, because I'm trying to do the exact same thing!'"

"I suggest that for the next few weeks, we take Angela Johnson as our mentor, our teacher, and we try to learn from her (because we're a lot like her). What do you think?" The children nodded with vigor.

Reread the author's work, pointing out that the author has written a text that is like what the children write. In this instance, Angela Johnson has written a Small-Moment story like those the children have been writing.

"I'm going to reread this book and this time when you listen, notice that it's a Small-Moment story just like the stories you've been writing." Amanda reread aloud *Joshua's Night Whispers*.

> In the nighttime the wind brings night whispers, so I follow them . . . past my toy box . . . and out my door . . . then down the hall. Night whispers all around. At last Daddy's holding me warm and safe and we listen together to the night whispers.

Amanda and I selected Angela Johnson because Joshua's Night Whispers *is a perfect exemplar text for Small Moment writing. We don't begin the unit by laying out all Angela Johnson's books and saying, "Go to it." Instead, we draw children close around this single text. If our author study had been Ezra Jack Keats, we'd focus similarly on* The Snowy Day *and if it was Donald Crews, we'd look at* Shortcut.

Amanda gets right to the heart of this unit and does so using simple, straight words. "I suggest we take Angela Johnson as our mentor." She doesn't detour into a long definition of mentor but does include a synonym at just the right moment.

We again tell children how we want them to listen before we read aloud in a minilesson.

Tell children that today they need to choose topics and get started on new pieces. Explain that when you have a mentor author (as they now have Angela Johnson), she teaches you lessons like how to choose topics and how to get started.

"We were on vacation so we missed writing workshop for two weeks. I know you all are dying to write. So, today we'll choose topics so we can start our new writing pieces. Today I want to teach you that a mentor author like Angela Johnson can give us tips on how to come up with ideas for writing."

Teaching

Tell children that Angela probably first thought of a big general topic and then decided to focus on a tiny aspect of that topic.

"I'm pretty sure that when Angela sits down to write (like we'll do soon) she probably has a few big, huge topics on her mind. I think of them as watermelon topics." Amanda used her hands to visually illustrate the big size of a watermelon topic. "She probably thinks 'I *could* write about my vacation'" Amanda's hands showed this would be a watermelon topic, "'or all about my son Joshua (another watermelon topic). . . .'"

"Angela could have written *everything* she had to say about Joshua: how he found an acorn that looked like a man on his walk yesterday, how he loved to make pancakes shaped like a *J*. . . ." Amanda's voice accentuated that this would have resulted in a scattered, on-and-on, list-like sort of piece. "But Angela decided not to write about a watermelon topic—like 'all about' her son—and instead she took just one tiny seed, one tiny topic. So she wrote just about the time when Joshua heard night noises and got out of bed."

You will want to decide how the author you have selected can help children with the very beginning of their writing process. You won't want to say, "Angela Johnson wrote about the sounds of one evening and you can write about night sounds too," because you are hoping children learn strategies (not topics) from authors they admire. You could help children emulate Angela's process of mining her ordinary home life for topics. Amanda decided to focus not on helping children know what they could write about, but on reminding them to zoom in on tiny, specific topics

This metaphor has been helpful in lots of K–1 classrooms, but a few children interpret the term watermelon topic literally and write about watermelons and seeds! Be mindful that metaphors can be confusing to children who are English language learners. Don't bypass metaphor, but do explicitly tell them what you mean. "You know how watermelons are big? Well, when I say a 'watermelon topic' I mean a big topic such as. . . ."

Tell children you think Angela Johnson probably uses a notepad to record the little details that later become stories.

"I'm pretty sure that to write this, Angela Johnson probably heard Joshua get out of bed in the night, and she probably said to herself, 'I could write about that.' Then she probably wrote the idea in a tiny topics notepad like this." Amanda held up a tiny spiral notepad. "Maybe she wrote 'Joshua—up in the night.' Then later when it was writing time, she probably saw the idea she'd written and thought, 'That'd make a good story!'"

Active Engagement

Ask children to think of a big topic and to tell that topic to their writing partners. Then ask them to think of one tiny, tiny story idea—one seed—inside that big watermelon topic.

"Right now, think of a big watermelon idea . . . my trip, my dog, playing with my friend, and tell that topic to your partner." They did so in twenty seconds. "Now think of a tiny, tiny seed idea, one detailed story inside that big *watermelon* idea. Angela's watermelon idea was to write about her son Joshua, and she actually wrote about the tiny, tiny topic (the size of a tiny seed) about one time when Joshua got out of bed because he heard night noises. She wrote that in her tiny topics notepad. Turn to your partner and tell your partner your tiny topic."

Alissa turned to Anthony, "I can write about how, when I went skating, the ice was slippery. I almost fell. My sister held my hand." She gestured to show how her outstretched arms helped her maintain her balance while skating.

"I am going to write about when I was with my dad in the park and I was trying to knock icicles down from the trees."

"Did you get any icicles?" Alissa asked, but before Anthony could answer, it was time to reconvene with the class.

It takes imagination for the author study to inform children's work because all we have to go on is the author's final text, not the author's process. This is okay because we can help children imagine what the author probably did to write. This works because we can surmise that the author probably did whatever it is we want our kids to do! Amanda and I emphasize the lifework of writing not because of our study of Angela Johnson but because we think that after a semester of writing in school, it is time for children's writing lives to spill over into their homes. We use the author study, then, as a forum for teaching that writers live differently.

Every unit of study adds a new tool, and each new tool becomes a concrete representation of that unit's new concept. During the revision unit, children had revision pens of a different color. Soon you'll give them tiny topic notepads and these will be concrete representations of the fact that writers consider the details of their lives worth noticing, and live differently because they write.

Whispering, Anthony said, "Yeah, 'cause my dad put me on his shoulders! Then I could reach."

Link

Show students that writers record their ideas. Give students tiny topics notepads in which to collect tiny details they might write about.

"I was thinking you all might want to live writerly lives just like Angela. I've got something very special for each of you." Amanda held up one of the tiny notepads. "Before we can write in these tiny topics notepads, we need to make them our very own, so I have a cover page that I'll give to each of you. Today let's decorate our covers, and then I'll attach the cover to your tiny topics notepad. If you have more time after that, you can open up your tiny topics notepad and write the story idea you just had or others. Then you can get a booklet and begin to write one of your stories."

"So let's fancy up these tiny topics notepads. Would the table monitor from the red table come and get your covers and notepads? The table monitor from the blue table. . . ."

Mid-Workshop Teaching Point

Intervene to remind children to jot ideas for topics in their notepads—and not to write whole stories there.

Once a few children had finished decorating their covers and were ready to write, Amanda reiterated what goes in the notepads. "Writers, may I stop you? Alissa's notepad is all set to go, and now she's going to write 'almost falling on the ice' on one page because that's one tiny topic she could write. She already wrote 'too small coat' because last night she tried on her winter coat and the sleeves came to here on her. So right on this page," Amanda said, holding up Alissa's notepad, "she wrote 'too small coat.' If she decides to turn that into a story, will she write the whole story here, in her tiny topics notepad?"

"Noooooo!"

"You're right. She'd get a booklet like this for her whole story, right?"

It is important to notice whether any children have taken your metaphor literally and are talking about watermelon and honeydew melon. If this happens, be patient and continue to move between the metaphor and the concrete meaning, as when you say, "Angela Johnson didn't write 'all about' her son, she didn't write about a huge watermelon-sized topic, did she?"

All the kids won't totally "get" the idea of what to put into the notepads (a phrase capturing their topic idea, as in "knocking down icicles") versus the four-page booklets (the Small-Moment story, like those they've written all year). You may need to confer or lead strategy lessons to help them. For now, they will have no trouble getting started decorating their covers.

As children complete the illustrations on the cover of their books, use clear packing tape to tape the covers onto the books in a way that effectively laminates them to the existing spiral notebook covers.

It is very important that the notepads are tiny. We often buy very small spirals (with wire loops along the side) and cut each of these into three even-tinier notepads. In the next session, we use lanyards to turn these into necklaces.

TIME TO CONFER

You will have your hands full today. For ten minutes, your children will be absorbed in an effort to decorate their covers. You can supervise and manage, supplying new pieces of construction paper to children who worry that they messed up their first efforts and taping completed covers onto the spirals. While you do this, talk up the purposes of the tool. "Once you're done, you'll want to carry this with you everywhere just like I do with my notepad. Yesterday, I was in the midst of patting my dog and all of a sudden I got an idea for a tiny topic." See the conferences cited at right from the *Conferring with Primary Writers* book.

As soon as children begin to write, you'll need to guard against them writing their whole stories in these notebooks. If you catch a child filling up page after page, that's a good sign that they're doing just that—race over immediately and remind the child to record just a note, rather than the whole story. If you don't do this, the notepad will be filled up in no time. If a lot of children reach this point, convene a strategy lesson or bring Session II's mid-workshop teaching point into today.

Most of your conferring time will be usurped by the mechanics of today, but if you have chances for real conferences, use the Small Moment conferences as guides.

These conferences in *The Conferring Handbook* may be especially helpful today:

▶ *"Will You Touch Each Page and Say What You'll Write?"*
▶ *"Let Me Help You Put Some Words Down"*
▶ *"As a Reader, I'd Love to Hear More About That"*

Also, if you have *Conferring with Primary Writers*, you may want to refer the following conferences:

▶ A Strategy Lesson on Keeping a Tiny-Topics Notepad
▶ "Are You Stuck?"

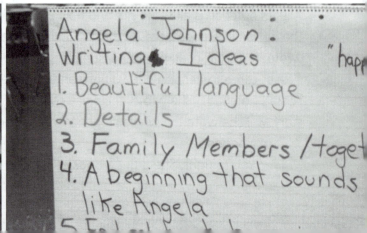

Angela Johnson:
Writing Ideas   "happ
1. Beautiful language
2. Details
3. Family Members /toget
4. A beginning that sounds
   like Angela
5.

AFTER-THE-WORKSHOP SHARE

Show the class the writing a few students did. Use these examples to teach how to use the tiny notepads

"Many of you have been showing me the tiny topics you recorded in your tiny topics notepad. We know Angela Johnson probably wrote, 'Joshua—up in the night' in her tiny topics notepad. Ben wrote, 'purring on the chair.' That note reminds him of a whole story about his cat coming to sleep beside him. Rachael wrote, 'Mom left' and that topic reminds her of a Small-Moment story about when she thought her Mom had left without saying good-bye. Eric wrote, 'cherry pie' and I can almost taste it right now!"

We actually don't have any evidence that Angela Johnson keeps a 2" x 1" notepad for topic ideas, but she's assured me that we can take this poetic license! Children benefit from multiple and very specific examples of the sort of thing you hope they will do.

POST-WORKSHOP TEACHING POINT

Convene students. Reread *Joshua's Night Whispers*. Have students talk with their partners about how Angela probably lived her life to write this book.

"Before you go, I'm going to reread Angela Johnson's *Joshua's Night Whispers* one more time. This time, I want you to think about the kind of life Angela probably lives to write like this because before you go home, I want you to think about living, tonight, like an author."

Have students think about how Angela Johnson lives her life in order to write as she does. Elicit a few responses.

Amanda read the book aloud. "What kind of life do you suppose she lives to write like this?"

Damon said, "It's a good story."

"Yes, it is a great story. But Damon, what I asked was this. What kind of life do you suppose Angela lives to write like this?"

"That she loves her family?"

"That's a smart observation. How do you suppose she remembers tiny moments like this one?"

"Maybe she puts stuff in a notepad to tell what her kid does."

Notice this is a Before-you-go-home minilesson! The architecture—connection, teaching, active engagement link—is almost, but not quite, present. At the start of this intervention, Amanda names what she'll teach and how this fits into their prior work.

We do children no favors if we ask a question and then accept responses that can't address the stated question. Notice how Amanda handles Damon's responses.

"Or maybe she sits in her house and thinks about Joshua."

"It's like she remembers everything. She remembers all the noises and places he went to find them."

Tell students what you heard them saying.

"I heard you guys say that Angela really loves her family and pays attention to them. She noticed how her son climbs out of bed to find the night noises. What Damon said is so true—it *is* like she remembers everything! Writers *do* find stories in the little everyday things like going to bed and waking up. They find stories in the morning sun, the lost mitten that no one can find when it is time to leave for school, and the walk in the rain with one's sister."

Remind students to watch for little things that could become stories and to record these in their tiny topics notepads.

"We're going to be leaving for home soon and tonight I have an assignment for you. I want you to live like writers. Today we learned that writers like Angela Johnson *write* with details because they *live* with details."

"Collect little, tiny details that you can later turn into stories. For example, earlier I looked at those bird tracks out our window and I wrote, 'bird footprints.' So tonight, look at the small things in your house and write a few that matter into your tiny topics notepads. Be like Angela Johnson. Listen and look closely. Tomorrow you'll all write with details because tonight you'll live with details."

Details convey worlds more than generalizations. Amanda says, "Writers find stories in the lost mitten . . . the walk in the rain . . ." rather than simply saying "Writers find stories in small details."

Notice that the Active Engagement phase of the minilesson is missing. Amanda is trying to set the children up to work well at home, but she wants this minilesson to go more quickly than the one earlier today.

The parallel construction in this sentence makes it easier to absorb. Writers write *with details because they* live *with details.*

Although most minilessons are tightly organized to introduce, demonstrate, and provide practice on a very specific skill, today's minilesson—like most first minilessons in a unit—instead provides a big-picture overview. You'll "unpack" this minilesson over the days that follow. Among other things:

▶ You'll want to keep your own tiny topics notepad and be very public about the times when you write in it. If the goldfish dies, tell children that you realize you could write a story about this and record it in your tiny topics notepad. If someone says something funny or sweet or worth remembering say, "Can you guys wait one second, I have to do something" and pull your notepad out without making an explicit lesson or obvious fuss over what you're doing. They'll notice all the more!

▶ Meanwhile, you can also give children opportunities throughout the day to identify watermelon topics and seed-like tiny topics for each other. When they come in from recess, say, "If Sophia wanted to write about recess, would that be a watermelon topic or a seed-like tiny topic? What about if she wrote about swinging so high she almost touched the tree branch—would that be a watermelon topic or a seed-like tiny topic?"

▶ The children's books mentioned in Getting Ready will fit perfectly into this minilesson. They are precious jewels—don't miss the chance to share them with your children.

STRETCHING SMALL MOMENTS, AS ANGELA MIGHT

GETTING READY

- *The Leaving Morning*
- Chart paper booklet
- Tiny topic notepads for each child, which they should already have from the previous minilesson
- Your own notepad with details jotted on a few pages
- Sharpened pencils, pens
- Lanyards or yarn (to turn the booklets into necklaces)
- Scissors, tape, staplers for revision
- Stapled booklets for writers, each containing four or five pages
- See CD-ROM for resources

CHILDREN WILL COME TO SCHOOL WITH TINY TOPICS, *tiny moments,* inscribed in their notepads. Your challenge will be to help them go from these jotted notes towards writing Small Moment stories. In the preceding unit, they devoted themselves to revising previously written texts, so it has been awhile since they've generated new pieces of writing. You hope to quickly remind them of the lessons they learned during your Small Moment study: to plan for how their stories will unfold across a series of pages, to write focused narratives, and to write with details.

Before today's minilesson, it will be important to have read The Leaving Morning to the class at least once. Today, when you reread it, talk with the class about what Angela Johnson may have written in her tiny topics notepad to jog her into remembering and writing this story.

In this session, you will use a portion of The Leaving Morning to show what it looks and sounds like when Angela Johnson tells the whole story of a tiny moment. Then you will help the youngsters turn their own jotted notes into Small Moment stories by demonstrating the process for them.

THE MINILESSON

Connection

Tell about one child who used his notepad the evening before to record a tiny detail. Remind children that writers not only *write* but also *live* with details.

"Earlier today we read *The Leaving Morning*, and some of you said Angela probably jotted 'moving morning' in her tiny topics notepad before she wrote this story. Yesterday, as we waited for the bus, Nathaniel said, 'I might write about sports,' and then he did a smart thing—he jotted down '3 strikes.' Today I will show you how to go from a tiny topic like '3 strikes' to a whole story. I want to remind you that writers don't just think up a topic and then suddenly write a story. Writers plan."

Teaching

Tell students that tiny topics need to grow in our minds before they are written.

"When Angela Johnson wrote *The Leaving Morning*, she may have gotten the idea for the book from a note she'd written about 'moving morning.' But her story didn't just barge right out. She first took her tiny topic and *let it grow in her mind*. She probably told the whole story to herself, or across her fingers, until it seemed right."

"See, like you, I already wrote some tiny topics in my notepad." Amanda held a page of her tiny spiral up for children to see. She read, 'buildings sparkling.' "Would you guys be researchers and watch what I do with the tiny topic I wrote in my notepad?"

"Researchers, watch. Before I write my story, it helps if I tell the story to myself. Sometimes I tell it across my fingers (remember how we used to do that?). Sometimes I turn the pages of the book and tell what goes on one page, the next, and the next. Sometimes I sketch the story out in a little box at the top of each of the pages. So either on my fingers or on the pages, I plan how the story will go. Watch me."

Amanda tells children that writers don't just think up a topic and write it, but instead they plan. Actually her goal is not just the sort of planning that writers do at their desks. Her goal is not deskwork, but lifework.

Amanda held up her fingers to remind students they can match each part of their story to one finger, as they learned in previous units. Actually, it's doubtful that Angela told this story across her fingers but it helps to suggest she may have! Keep in mind that whether children tell their story across their fingers or by touching each page of a blank booklet and saying what they might write, the big lesson is that writers rehearse for writing.

"Hmm. Okay. I want to tell . . . I have to think what the whole story will mainly be. Hmm. . . ." Now Amanda held out a clenched hand and opened one finger at a time as she told this story: "Remember when we did this earlier in the year?"

The rain had just stopped.
I was sitting on the cross-town bus, staring out the window, watching the sky turn pale blue.
I saw people open their jackets. I saw puddles misting in the sun.
Suddenly I looked up and all around me the buildings were sparkling.

"See how I took a tiny topic and I am planning it as a story?"

Active Engagement

Ask the class to take an idea you'd recorded earlier in the day and grow it into a story, tellng the story to a partner.

"Let's try one together. Remember when we found our blue fish, belly up? Remember how I wrote that in my tiny topics notepad, 'belly up fish.' Pretend *you* wrote that and that now you have decided to make a story out of that belly up fish. Tell it across your fingers. Partner one, tell the story to partner two. Start with an action. What did you do or hear or notice first?"

Link

Remind children how Angela Johnson might have gotten the idea for her story, emphasizing they can do the same—they can find and record tiny moments.

"Today, and every day, you'll find tiny topics in your lives. When you go from a tiny topic to a story—remember to give your story time to grow."

MID-WORKSHOP TEACHING POINT

Tell students a quick story of a child who remembered to write in her tiny topics notepad even in the middle of something else.

"While we've been writing, Tashika just lost her tooth. She is in the middle of another story, but she didn't want to forget about the tooth, so she jotted it in her tiny topics notepad. Some of the rest of you may find things happening to you, or come to your mind, as you're writing—and I know you'll use your tiny topics notepad."

Amanda doesn't just explain that she first wrote a topic, then wrote a story. She instead reenacts the process, starting with the words "Watch me." Reenacting (or dramatizing) gives children a demonstration. Demonstrations are vastly more effective than explanations.

Amanda has set the children up to try the very thing she's described. There are no machinations—children are set to go and can simply turn to their partner and start. It isn't necessary for children to report back. The point is to give them a minute to try something.

Amanda is using beautiful metaphor to describe the writing process. She may want to convene her English language learners and to be more explicit about what she means when she says "give your story time to grow."

TIME TO CONFER

For now, your conferences will resemble those from *Small Moments* and *Writing for Readers*. You'll help children focus on small moments, make movies in their minds, and retell their stories. You'll watch for children who talk about something they've done, rather than retelling a detailed narrative of the incident. If they summarize rather than story-tell, try saying, "Can you picture exactly what happened? How did it start? What did you do (or say) first?" Let them respond, then repeat it back in a storytelling way, and elicit more. "Then what?" If some of your children's narratives sound like lists: "I go to the park. I go roller skating. I go on the ramp. I come home," you could:

- Explicitly teach children that when writers write stories, we sometimes use connecting words such as *then, later, a few minutes later, afterwards, suddenly, after,* and so on. These words could be charted.
- Be sure children rehearse their stories by touching each page and saying aloud the words they'll write. You might restate what the child says using more story-like language. If the child says "I go to the park," you might ask, "When did you go?" After learning the time, you might show the child how to combine the time and the action. "Say that, 'Yesterday I went skating in the park.'"

Whatever you nudge children to do, make a connection to Angela Johnson. You may say, "Write that story down! Then you'll have a book, just like Angela Johnson" or "Write those details. Your story will be as detailed as *Joshua's Night Whispers*."

These conferences in *The Conferring Handbook* may be especially helpful today:

- *"Will You Touch Each Page and Say What You'll Write?"*
- *"Let Me Help You Put Some Words Down"*
- *"As a Reader, I'd Love to Hear More About That"*

Also, if you have *Conferring with Primary Writers*, you may want to refer the conferences in part five.

AFTER-THE-WORKSHOP SHARE

Tell students the story of a child who planned her Small Moments story across her fingers before writing it.

"Listen to what Penny did today. She had written, 'doing Sara's hair,' in her tiny topics notepad to remind her how she does her little sister's hair in the mornings. But she didn't just write that story straight away. Instead she remembered that Angela Johnson lets her seed idea *grow in her mind* before she started writing. When she wrote *The Leaving Morning*, Angela Johnson kept thinking and thinking until she had a whole story about the leaving morning, starting with the street sweeper, and the boxes of clothes.

"So Penny told *her* story across her fingers before she started writing. Instead of just saying, 'I do Sara's hair,' her story starts, 'Sara stood on the stool by the mirror. Her hair had knots in it. I brushed the knots. I put barrettes in Sara's hair.' Don't you love how the planning part helped Penny get details into her story!"

You may want to give another, short example.

"And look what Elizabeth has done. She started with a jotted note in her tiny topics notepad and then she wrote this story. Listen." [*Fig. II-1*]

Ask children to tell their partners their Small-Moments stories across their fingers to their partners.

"Will you guys share your tiny topic with your partner and tell your partner the story you are writing? Tell the story across your fingers, or by touching each page and saying the words that might go on that page."

Me and my mom went to catch and see fireflies. Once when I was three years old me and my mom went to catch fireflies. We waited a little until the fireflies came. Then we saw them! Their lights were glowing bright. My mom caught one. I tried to catch one also. Then suddenly I caught one. I yelled out! Then we caught more and more. We would let them go each time we caught them. Then we would watch them all go. Then we would go home, go to bed, and dream about fireflies.

Fig. II-1   Elizabeth

POST-WORKSHOP TEACHING POINT

Encourage children to gather ideas for writing and take notes all day long.

"Some of you were asking if you could carry your tiny topics notepad around with you at lunch and on the playground to write down more tiny details that you don't want to forget. That's a good idea. I'll help you turn your notepads into necklaces so you can carry them everywhere."

ANOTHER POST-WORKSHOP TEACHING POINT

Remind children to jot down details for their writing in their tiny notepads.

"Writers, as you go home tonight, plan to live like writers again, jotting ideas for stories in your tiny topics notepad. Angela didn't write 'Joshua' but instead jotted a tiny detail in her notepad. Listen to Byrd Baylor's advice. Pay attention to the small things."

Do this: With a mountain.
Go get to know   Don't start
One thing as well   With the whole
As you can.   Pacific Ocean.
                            Start with:
It should be   One seed pod
Something   Or
Small.   One horned toad
                            Or
Don't start   One Handful Of Dirt

"She *could* have said, 'Start with one night whisper, with one kiss on the window pane, or one leaving morning,' couldn't she have? We all need to take lessons from these details in Angela Johnson's writing."

Sometimes we'll make a comment like this regardless of whether it is exactly true. Jerome Harste once said, "I see curriculum as creating in the classroom the kind of world we believe in and then helping children role play their ways into being the readers and writers we want them to be."

Byrd Baylor's book, The Other Way to Listen, *is filled with spectacular excerpts such as this one.*

Students can use yarn or lanyards to string their notepads into necklaces. It helps if the lace goes through three of the top spirals of the tiny topics notepad and continues around the child's neck. New materials are a major source of motivation for little children, so parse the new materials out bit-by-bit when the time is right. The necklaces make the notepads more portable so it's perfect to bring this adaptation now.

IF CHILDREN NEED MORE TIME

We expect you'll plan and lead at least one and probably several minilessons that sustain this focus for a bit longer. Remember that you are also teaching during conferences, strategy lessons, and share sessions. In any of these teaching forums, you might use one or more of these ideas.

▶ Share a child's jotted topic and then the story written from that topic. Tell the story behind the work.

▶ Use a book the children know well and speculate how it came into existence. "This book probably started when the author. . . ."

▶ A number of authors have written beautifully about the writerly life, and snippets of their work can be woven into minilessons. These are our all-time favorites:

The Other Way to Listen	Byrd Baylor
I'm in Charge of the Celebration	Byrd Baylor
The Wise Woman and Her Secret	Eve Merriam

▶ To create other minilessons on living the writerly life, you may want to read *The Art of Teaching Writing* (Calkins) Chapters 3, 27, 29; *Living Between the Lines* (Calkins with Harwayne), Chapters 2, 4; or *What a Writer Needs* (Fletcher), Chapter 4.

Most of your whole-class teaching energy right now will be devoted to your effort to launch new aspects of this unit. You'll try to sweep children up in an excitement over Angela Johnson's books and you'll encourage children to live writerly lives, seeing possible topics for writing everywhere. But meanwhile, when you have a chance to bring children's folders home, you'll want to look at each child's writing journey since the start of school.

Look at the fundamentals of writing. Think about each child in relationship to your goals for the year. Above all, look at the changes you can see in each child's writing. Some children are far more proficient as writers than others; the question that matters most is whether every child has made dramatic, obvious progress.

If your children have been involved in a daily writing workshop as described here, you should see that most are writing more and more conventionally. Be sure their paper choices change along with the children. Study the student texts included in this book and notice how the options for paper choice have changed.

You'll probably find that a few children have not progressed like the others. Begin to spend time each day with these children. If some children aren't using enough sound-letter connections to be able to reread their own writing (or if they aren't leaving spaces between words), you can let their author study work be carried along by the class's energy. Meanwhile, you'll want to focus all your conferences and strategy lessons with these children on these foundational aspects of writing. Remember that the minilessons for *Writing for Readers* can be tweaked and repeated as small-group strategy lessons for children needing this sort of support.

STUDYING ANGELA'S WRITING: ELLIPSES CREATE DRAMATIC TENSION

GETTING READY

- Copies of Angela Johnson's books they've read thus far (transcripts or individual copies of the books for each child or pair of children)
- Writing folders to fill with writing from this unit
- Begin "Craft" chart (size of bulletin board)
- Enlarged copy of *Joshua's Night Whispers* (one way to do this is to make an overhead transparency of each page and to project it)
- See CD-ROM for resources

WE HAVE BEEN HELPING STUDENTS LIVE WRITERLY LIVES, *as Angela Johnson does. Now we will help students emulate her writing techniques. Your children will create a chart of ways Angela writes. The chart you'll make is an adaptation of Katie Ray's in* Wondrous Words. *You will help students describe exactly what Johnson has done to write a good story, find further examples of this technique, and speculate about the reasons for using it. In the end, we hope children try Angela's techniques in their own writing.*

Joshua's Night Whispers *is a perfect text for this study. It is only forty-three words, but if children study this little book, they'll see a surprising number of admirable features—and learn the value of looking closely. You are inviting children to develop a never-ending resource, books, that can enrich their own writing for years to come. First children must learn how to notice evidence of craftsmanship in a text. For some, it will be new to think not only about* what *a text says but also about* how *the text is written. You'll need to welcome children's rough approximations, knowing the lessons you teach in the next few days will continue to challenge children for years.*

Your minilessons will be unusual this week. You'll elicit more from your children, tell them less, and offer more in response to what they say. The teaching and active involvement components will be combined, and the minilessons will be longer than usual.

In this session, you will coach students to find and think about a special feature that they notice in Angela Johnson's stories.

The Minilesson

Connection

Tell students that this week, they'll revise their writing using Angela Johnson as a teacher-of-revision.

"Today, we have reached a new chapter in our work. Remember how, in December, we found stories that deserved to be revised? We put them in special revision folders and then revised them? Well, today we're going to put the stories we've been writing over the last few days into our revision folders and we will begin revising them. But this time we are going to let Angela Johnson be our revision teacher. We are going to try the same moves that she makes."

"Have you ever watched a great sports player—a great baseball player or a skateboarder—and then tried to do the same as the pro? That's what we'll continue to do this week, but our pro will be a writer."

Teaching and Active Engagement

Distribute copies of *Joshua's Night Whispers*. Ask children to listen and look while you read the text and then to tell their partners what Angela Johnson does as a writer.

"Today, let's study the way Angela Johnson writes her book, *Joshua's Night Whispers*. I have a copy of the story for each of you. Look carefully at the text and tell your partner what you notice Angela Johnson does as a writer." I passed out the copies and listened in on their conversations. "Okay, so what are some of the things you noticed Angela Johnson has done in *Joshua's Night Whispers*?" I called children together to focus on a copy of the text, which I'd enlarged using an overhead projector.

The medium is the message for youngsters. Transporting the children's revision folders from December's unit into this unit helps transport December's revision strategies into January's writing workshop.

It's easier for young children to write a few books, then revise a few books, rather than to shuttle back and forth between drafting and revision. And it's easier for children to focus on implementing a particular writing technique if they are revising (keeping just that one technique in mind) rather than if they are trying to draft with their attention split between content and craft.

When you invite children to study a text, and to name what the author has done, you need to be prepared to follow your children's lead. Chances are good that your children (like these) will notice ellipses (among other things), but they may lead you down another path. . . .

Jordan pointed: "She puts a comma there."

San Hoi: "She planned out her story and wrote with good words."

Danielle: "She puts spaces."

Missy: "She tells what Joshua goes past on the way."

Kelsea: "She uses lots of punctuation, like three periods."

Manuel: "She uses the three dots in two places."

"Hmmm. She uses three dots together in two different places? Why do you think she does that?"

Emma: "To make it sound right."

San Hoi: "So you stop for three seconds."

"It is so interesting to think why she uses these three dots, isn't it? So San Hoi, you think it makes you stop for three seconds? Why would she want us to stop? Let me reread it and let's think. Why does Angela Johnson want us to stop?" I read the text, allowing the ellipses to create drama and suspense.

Elizabeth: "There's going to be something exciting."

Dylan: "Yeah, like something scary is going to happen. To let you know to slow down because something is going to happen."

Isabelle: "I always use dot, dot, dot when something is going to happen."

Mohammed: "More is coming."

"These are such interesting ideas. I think I see what you mean." I reread the story emphasizing the suspense that accompanies the ellipses. "You're right. Each time there were three dots, I wondered what was going to happen next. I was so glad when Joshua finally reaches his daddy!"

Show and explain to the students what the "Craft" chart is and how it will help us be better writers. Begin to fill it with student input.

"To help us keep track of what we notice as we study Angela Johnson's writing, I've made a special chart, a 'Craft' chart. There is a section called, *Where?* for us to name the book, and then *What do you see?* and one called *Why is she doing this?* and the last sections are, We *call it . . .* and *Other books?* Let's try filling it out together."

I decide which of their observations to "get behind." In this instance, I support the ellipses because every child can notice ellipses and can incorporate them into one of their pieces. The downside of this is that ellipses can take over your children's writing, and they aren't necessarily a great boon to the quality of writing. I've come to anticipate that young children tend to notice concrete, localized features, such as ellipses or sound effects, and to realize I can usually engineer my teaching so that these very concrete features in a text come to represent larger qualities of good writing. For example, ellipses are a way in which Angela Johnson builds drama and suspense in her story, and tension and drama are important aspects of a story.

Notice that this minilesson relies on children's input more than most. Our goal is to teach children that they can study texts and identify features worth emulating.

Here I try to link ellipses with dramatic tension.

Where?	What do you see?	Why is she doing this?	We call it . . .	Other Books?
Joshua's Night Whispers				

For now, I will scaffold work with this chart heavily. First- and second-grade children will have opportunities later on in the unit to work with this chart more independently.

"So we can start by writing the title in the first column. For this next section, *What do you see?* several of you noticed that she uses three dots together and Manuel said she uses this in two different places." I pointed two places out and the children noticed a third place. "So here (in column two,) I'll write '3 dots, 3 times.'"

"The next column says, '*Why is she doing this?*' Dylan, I wrote down in my spiral what you said, 'She lets the reader know to slow down because something more is going to happen.' Here, I'll write 'slows reader down, something more is going to happen.' The ellipses or three dots add suspense, don't they? Now, what shall we name this thing that Angela does so we all know what it is we are talking about?"

Notice that I am not even attempting to elicit much of this from the kids. Today I'm content to demonstrate—and I save huge moments of time by making moves such as when I say, "Dylan . . . earlier you said . . . so let's write . . . here."

Manuel raised his hand. "I know, I know! We can call it 'happening punctuation.'"

Mohammed, also eager to participate, added, "Or dot, dot, dot."

"What do you think?" Soon the class agreed to name this strategy "Dot, dot, dot."

I don't love the title "happening punctuation" because it seems vague. That's why I ask for other input from others in the class. I don't need to name this "dot, dot, dot," but I do hope for a title that will work as a short-cut to call to mind the admirable feature.

I wrote that on the chart.

Where?	What do you see?	Why is she doing this?	We call it . . .	Other Books?
Joshua's Night Whispers	3 dots, 3 times	Slows reader down, something more is going to happen	Dot, dot, dot.	

Link

As you send students off, suggest to them that some may want to analyze and reread _The Leaving Morning_ to see if Angela Johnson does anything similar in that book.

"Today, during writing workshop, some of you may want to look at _The Leaving Morning_ and see if Angela does any of those same things there. Maybe one or two of you will actually try to use Angela Johnson's techniques in your writing."

Some children will probably be able to read The Leaving Morning. _For others, you'll need to create a small group to listen to and talk about it._

The Leaving Morning incorporates most of the writerly techniques a student would notice in Joshua's Night Whispers. _Children will be unbelievably excited if you let them discover the parallels on their own—you will have set them up for success._

TIME TO CONFER

Energy will be sky-high today. If some of your children can read *The Leaving Morning*, you'll see huddles of kids pulled close around that book, and they won't be able to contain their excitement when they find that this book incorporates ellipses just as the children have seen in *Joshua's Night Whispers*. See conference cited at right.

Act amazed (like you never saw this until now) when they race over to show you that they have discovered parallel craft moves between the two books. You can channel their energy towards noticing more parallels between the texts (there are zillions) or you can encourage the writers to see if they, too, want to try this strategy. Meanwhile, notice what children are doing and keep records of it on your conferring checklist. This checklist should help you have the eyes to see and to celebrate what they are doing, or are almost doing.

In an author study unit, don't be surprised if you look around during the writing workshop and see that everyone is *reading* rather than *writing*. Your conferences, too, will support children's reading as well as their writing.

This conference in *The Conferring Handbook* may be especially helpful today:

▶ *"You Can Use Ellipses to Show Waiting"*

Also, if you have *Conferring with Primary Writers*, you may want to refer to the conferences in part five.

After-the-Workshop Share

Remind children of what many of them were attempting to do in writing workshop today. Ask them to share their work with their partners.

"I noticed that so many of you were trying out 'dot, dot, dot' in your writing. Some kids tried to use it to slow down their writing and make us wonder what was going to happen next. Can we share with our partner what we did in writing workshop today? Partner one, read your work first and show your partner what you tried today to do as a writer. Then partner two."

Read children an example of a child who tried the idea from the minilesson.

"Writers, let me stop you. I want to read Justin's piece to you. You'll be able to tell from my voice when Justin borrowed Angela Johnson's idea and used 'dot, dot, dots' to build up the feelings at certain times in his story." [*Fig. III-1*]

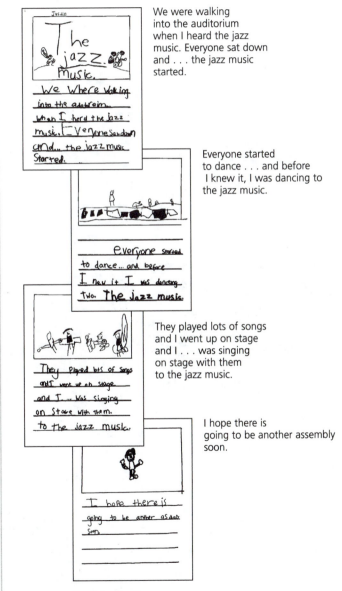

We were walking into the auditorium when I heard the jazz music. Everyone sat down and . . . the jazz music started.

Everyone started to dance . . . and before I knew it, I was dancing to the jazz music.

They played lots of songs and I went up on stage and I . . . was singing on stage with them to the jazz music.

I hope there is going to be another assembly soon.

Fig. III-1   Justin

LEARNING FROM ANGELA: WRITING WITH ELLIPSES

GETTING READY

▶ Your own story on chart paper

▶ Student writing on chart paper

▶ Craft chart visible to the children

● See CD-ROM for resources

WE BEGAN WITH AN OBVIOUS CRAFT TECHNIQUE *because it was so obvious. Most or all of the class will quickly notice Angela Johnson's use of ellipses, and they will be eager to try these in their own writing. This gets children into the swing of noticing an author's craft and of deliberately emulating what another writer has done.*

"Aren't there more important qualities of good writing to teach?" you might ask. It's true that many of the craft techniques that children are apt to spot (repetition, sound effects, speech bubbles, ellipses) aren't the most important qualities of good writing. However, half of our goal is to teach children the process of noticing what other authors have done in their texts. We want students to read and to think, "I could try that in my writing." Furthermore, most of the seemingly superficial things students notice are actually related to significant qualities of good writing. For example, as mentioned earlier, Angela Johnson uses ellipses to build tension in her simple story. Learning to write with ellipses can be a multilevel skill; kids can learn to use this punctuation mark simply or to begin learning about a larger part of writing: creating suspense.

In this session, you will coach children to incorporate a feature into their own writing that they've admired in Angela's writing: ellipses.

Connection

Tell children that today they will try to use techniques Angela Johnson has taught them. Do this in your own writing to demonstrate how one does this.

"Yesterday we started looking really closely at how Angela Johnson writes and we noticed she uses three dots together to slow us down and let us know something more will be happening. Whenever you see an author doing something you admire, you can say to yourself, 'I'm going to try that in *my* writing.' Today I'm going to show you how you can use "dot, dot, dot" in your own writing."

In the connection section of a minilesson, we essentially say to children, "Today I'm going to teach you one thing that good writers do often." I try to say explicitly that the one thing writers do often, that I hope children emulate, is admire and emulate the techniques of other authors. The specific use of "dot, dot, dot" is only a case in point.

Teaching

Read your story aloud. Think aloud as you make decisions about where you can add ellipses to your writing.

"As I read my story, I am going to think about if there are any places where I might try the 'dot, dot, dot' strategy Angela uses." Amanda read her story, slightly exaggerating a place where she wanted to add in ellipses.

The rain had just stopped.
I was sitting on the cross-town bus, staring out the window, watching the sky turn pale blue.
I saw people open their jackets. I saw puddles misting in the sun.
Suddenly I looked up and all around me the buildings were sparkling.

A chorus of "there, there" erupted.

"You think so?" Amanda reread her last sentence. "Where exactly? Like this?"

Suddenly I looked up and all around me the buildings were sparkling.

Soon the children had tried out several alternate spots and chosen one.

In this unit of study, a few texts reappear in many minilessons: Angela Johnson's books, this story of Amanda's, and the Craft chart. Whenever we plan a unit of study, we ask ourselves, "Which texts will thread through this unit?"

The rain had just stopped.
I was sitting on the cross-town bus, staring out the window, watching the
sky turn pale blue.
I saw people open their jackets. I saw puddles misting in the sun. . . .
Suddenly I looked up . . . and all around me the buildings were sparkling.

"It works, doesn't it? It's a lot like what Angela does in *Joshua's Night Whispers* when she has Joshua going down the hall, isn't it? She doesn't rush it either."

Active Engagement

Read one child's writing and ask the children to talk with their partners about where they would put in ellipses.

"You can do this too! Samantha wrote this story and I thought maybe you could help her figure out where she could put ellipses. I'll read it and you follow along. Then tell your partner where you think Samantha could add ellipses and why."

My friend was coming to visit from far away.
I went to the airport to pick her up.
I waited and waited and waited.
Finally, she came off the plane and I ran to give her a hug.

"So where do you think Samantha could have put ellipses to make her story go slower? Where would they make sense?"

Turning to her partner, Leslie said, "After 'my friend.'"

"No," Jose said. "Then it'd go, 'My friend . . . was coming. . . .' I think it should be after the word 'waited.'"

Listen in to the partnerships. Share one partnership's thinking with the class.

Amanda convened the group. "I just heard Jose suggest that the piece could go, 'I waited . . . and waited . . . and waited. . . .' Does that sound like a good place?"

The children chorused, "Yeees."

The crucial thing will be to read this little story in ways that emphasize that the ellipses affect the pace and tone of your voice.

Our minilessons allow us to demonstrate something and then give scaffolded practice doing the very thing we've demonstrated. This story was chosen because it practically begs for ellipses and Amanda reads it aloud in a way that helps children imagine places where ellipses might help. Consequently, it's much easier for children to add ellipses into this story than it will be for them to add ellipses into their own writing. This is as it should be. First we demonstrate something; then we give children scaffolded practice trying to do the same thing; finally we send children off to work more independently.

The children could have decided instead to use ellipses after "finally."

Link

Ask children to try writing with ellipses today. Suggest that others may try other strategies and techniques that interest them.

"Who is ready to try using 'dot, dot, dot' today in their writing? Great! When you try it, let me know. We'll talk about how it worked for some of you during our share time. Meanwhile, it'd be really wonderful if some of you noticed other things that Angela Johnson has done that you could try."

Whenever possible, leave children with options. There is no reason why every child must use ellipses today.

TIME TO CONFER

There will be days when the content of your minilesson is so complicated that your conferences adhere closely to your minilesson. Today will not be such a day! Children will take to ellipses with ease and enthusiasm. Instead of persevering with ellipses, take this opportunity to remind children that minilessons accumulate, and that anything you've ever taught should inform them as they work. Help children remember to write with focus, detail, dialogue, setting, character development, and clarity.

If you *do* want to confer about ellipses, help some children realize that ellipses work best if there is a part of the story where the character is trying, trying, trying to do something. If the story goes, "Today I put on my skates and soon I was skating in circles," there's not a lot of reason to use ellipses. But there are lots of places for ellipses in a story that goes, "I put on my skates. I stood wobbling for a moment . . . and fell. Again I stood. I wobbled. I started to skate . . . and again I fell." In this way, ellipses become an entryway into writing with dramatic tension. See the conference cited at right from the *Conferring with Primary Writers* book.

You will probably also help some children realize that ellipses don't necessarily belong in every piece, let alone every sentence!

These conferences in *The Conferring Handbook* may be especially helpful today:

▶ *"You Can Use Ellipses to Show Waiting"*
▶ *"Use a Refrain"*
▶ *"I See You're Adding an Exclamation Mark to Your Story Like Mem Fox Does"*

Also, if you have *Conferring with Primary Writers*, you may want to refer to the following conference:

▶ "But How Did You Feel in Your Story?"

After-the-Workshop Share

Celebrate the attempts children have made to use ellipses the way Angela does.

"You guys are so much like Angela! When I walked around today, I saw you using ellipses to slow your readers down, which is just what we saw Angela doing in her books. Pedro put them after he wrote, 'we climbed and we climbed and we climbed . . .' so we readers slow down when we get to that part and feel how high the hill was. Toby put them after he wrote, 'San Francisco is very far . . .' so we slow down and feel how far away his mom was when she went on her business trip, and how much he missed her. Toby and Pedro, can you hold up your stories so we can all see how you are writing just like Angela?"

Remind students to use ellipses carefully.

"But I want to remind you that we don't just put ellipses everywhere! We have to really think about where it would make sense for the reader to read slowly, in a bit-by-bit sort of way. Ellipses tell readers how to read our writing."

Have the whole class help one child think through the decisions of how to use ellipses.

"Jordan was just about to do something really smart when it was time to stop writing. So I though maybe we could help him. He was about to reread his piece and see if he likes how he's added 'dot, dot, dot.' Let's all help. I'll read aloud his piece and I'll tell you when he's written 'dot, dot, dot.' I'll read it twice, and the second time, after each 'dot, dot, dot,' will you let Jordan know whether you'd keep that ellipses (thumbs up) or take them out (thumbs down). Listen as I read the story." [*Fig. IV-1*]

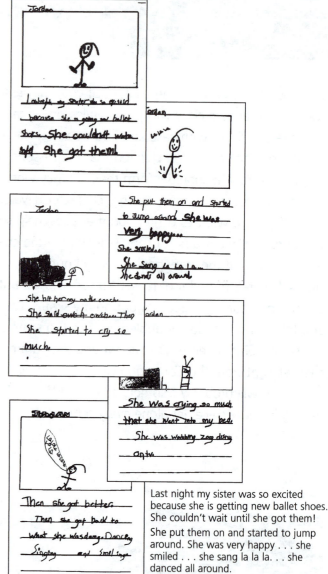

Fig. IV-1   Jordan

Last night my sister was so excited because she is getting new ballet shoes. She couldn't wait until she got them!

She put them on and started to jump around. She was very happy . . . she smiled . . . she sang la la la. . . . she danced all around.

She hit her knee on the couch. She said ouch . . . then she started to cry so much.

She was crying so much that she went into my bed. She was watching Zoog Disney on TV.

Then she got better. Then she got back to what she was doing. Dancing, singing and smiling.

IF CHILDREN NEED MORE TIME

This is probably not a minilesson that will need reiteration; in fact, you'll want to move away from ellipses to other observations soon or you'll regret ever mentioning them! If, however, by some chance, you want to do a strategy lesson with a few children who need more convincing, you might try the following:

▸ Look at the other text, *The Leaving Morning*, and examine how Angela Johnson uses ellipses in this story. Does she use them as often?

▸ Show a child who tried to be like Angela and wrote ellipses in his or her story. Ask the class to talk about the differences in the story before and after the ellipses were added.

▸ Read Angela's text (or another text with powerful ellipses) without ellipses so the children can hear the difference ellipses make.

▸ Read a child's booklet such as Elizabeth's *Main Rainbow* and see if listeners can hear where the author used ellipses and if they can say why she used them. [*Fig. IV-2*]

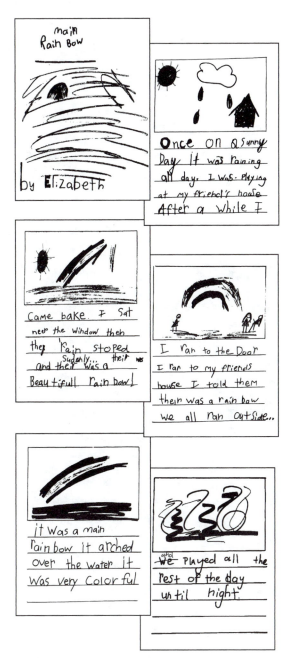

Fig. IV-2   Elizabeth

STUDYING ANGELA'S WRITING: COMEBACK LINES

GETTING READY

▶ *Joshua's Night Whispers* (transcripts or individual copies of the books for each child or pair of children)

▶ Enlarged copy of *Joshua's Night Whispers* (one way to do this is to make an overhead transparency of each page and to project it)

▶ *The Leaving Morning*

▶ Craft chart

▶ Other Angela Johnson books, including, if possible: *Joshua by the Sea; Mama Bird, Baby Birds; One of Three; Rain Feet;* and *When I Am Old with You*

● See CD-ROM for resources

So far in this unit, you have introduced children to a new way of working with texts and a new chart. It's important to continue working with these consistently. In this session, you'll bring children back to the very short text of Joshua's Night Whispers *and help them see much more. You can't plan what children will notice, but you can plan on giving them time to notice.*

This unit helps children go from seeing the most obvious feature of a mentor text (such as the ellipses) to seeing the less obvious, perhaps more significant traits. It will be important for you to work with whatever your kids see. Don't expect that just because we saw ellipses and repeating lines (as you'll see in this session) that your children will see the same.

Natalie's class noticed instead that Angela Johnson did something to make every page of her writing special. What a wonderful thing it was for these youngsters to study each page of Angela's writing to notice the evidence of craftsmanship, and then for them to try to do likewise on each and every page of their writing! These children added their own spectacular twist to this unit of study, and yours will do the same.

In this session, using the same chart as before and going back to the same book, you'll coach children to notice deeper, more embedded traits of Angela's writing. In this case, the children with whom Amanda and I work noticed the "comeback lines" in Angela Johnson's books.

The Minilesson

Connection

Tell children that they can learn many strategies from an author and use these in their writing.

"Yesterday many of us were trying to be like our mentor author by using 'dot, dot, dot' in our own writing. We can learn many things from Angela Johnson, or from any author, and we can try these things out in our own writing. When you notice that an author does something in his or her writing that you admire, you can try the same technique."

Teaching and Active Engagement

Invite children to return to the same brief text and learn more lessons from it.

"Today, let's closely study the way Angela Johnson writes her book, *Joshua's Night Whispers*. I've made copies of the book for each of you. Let's read the book and you follow along. I want you to be thinking about what you notice in her writing." I read the book aloud.

"What do you notice about her writing? Turn and tell your partner."

Anna: "She says 'night whispers' a lot in her story and that is the name of the story."

Rachael: "Yeah, and she uses special words, like 'night whispers.'"

Reconvene the class and ask what children noticed. Help students to name what Angela Johnson does and to speculate about why she does it.

"So what did you notice?"

"She says 'night whispers' a lot in her story and that's the name of the story," Anna announced with a flourish.

Notice that I refer to authors in general, rather than just to this author. For example, I say, "We were trying to be like our mentor author," or "We can learn many things from Angela Johnson, or from any author." I am trying, in subtle ways, to be sure that my students learn that they can study and emulate any author. If this whole month were devoted solely to a study of one author's craft techniques, I'd worry that our point wasn't worthy of the time we were investing.

I want to be sure that every child actually makes and collects observations about this text.

"You know what? You're right! Wow! Can you show us spots where she writes, 'night whispers' in the story?"

Anna pointed out two "night whispers" on the enlarged version of the story.

"Angela Johnson puts the title into the story? She does it two times? Anywhere else?"

Soon the other children found the same phrase was actually repeated *four* times in this forty-three-word text.

"So *why* do you think she writes the title over and over again in her story?"

If a child names what the author has done, give the child the ultimate compliment of learning from the child's observation, as I do when I say, "You know what? You're right! Wow!" instead of complimenting the child for the right answer (for example, "Good for you"). You could also follow up by asking, "Where do you see that?" Ask as if the child is informing you and others (rather than asking the child in a "Can you guess the right answer?" sort of way).

Let children discover this—don't take them directly to this realization. The working-it-out phase is incredibly good for them—as is the exultation of discovering a pattern!

When we see that an author has used the same technique in various places, we can begin to envision the technique as transferable to our own texts. In any author study, even if the author doesn't use the technique multiple times in one text, I ask students to find other instances of the same technique by asking, "Where else have you seen an author use this technique?"

It should be predictable that children notice something an author has done, then look to see if the author used that technique more than once. Then they speculate, "Why might the author have done this?" One way to draw this out is to ask, "How would the story have been different if she hadn't done whatever she did (in this instance, if she hadn't repeated the phrase 'night whispers')?"

Crafting techniques, in and of themselves, aren't good or bad. It could be problematic for an author to say the same words many times in a story, but Angela uses repetition for a reason. It helps to ask, "Why do you think the author did that?" The response to the question is less important than that they reflect on the question in the first place.

"Maybe she couldn't think of other ways."

"Maybe she liked the words so she put them there a lot."

"'Cause they're nice."

"Maybe because 'night whispers, night whispers,' that's the main thing in the story."

Refer to the chart to anchor the conversation. Say, "So far you've said …" and repeat what will go in the first columns of the chart. Then, shift the discussion to a later column.

I listened as if the children were each teaching each other and me—that is, I didn't listen in a "yes, you are saying what I thought all along" way. "So *one* thing Angela does as a writer is that she says the title over and over," I gestured to column two on the chart,"and she does this because those words are what the story is mainly about?" I then gestured to column three.

Where?	What do you see?	Why is she doing this?	We call it . . .	Other Books?
Joshua's Night Whispers	3 dots, 3 times	Slows reader down, something more is going to happen	Dot, dot, dot.	*The Leaving Morning*
				Our Stories
Joshua's Night Whispers				

"She uses 'night whispers' here," Juan continued, ignoring my question and reiterating what had already been said as he pointed to the title. "And here."

"'Cause they keep happening."

"So you're saying she keeps using that phrase because *in Joshua's real life, the night whispers kept coming*? Wow! And because night whispers are the main idea in her story. What ideas!" Now I pointed to the fourth column on the chart. "What do you think we should call it when an author repeats some words because they say what the story is mainly about?"

Be silent. Don't judge their response. Listen to it. Act interested, as if you are learning from them. Avoid calling on child after child. Let your eyes do that.

Notice whether children are speaking to the whole class. If a child seems to be telling you and only you his or her observation, gesture to the class. Say, "You're telling the class," and once the child has spoken you may say to the class, "What do you think? Do you agree or disagree? Would someone like to add on or talk back to that?"

Children gave lots of reasons why Angela may have repeated a phrase, and you'll see that I support just one of those reasons. I believe that, in general, if children are going to use refrains in their books, it'll help if those refrains capture the main idea of the text.

This was an astonishing comment that could have gone by me if I wasn't really listening to the kids. As we listen, we teach the class to listen. As we all listen together, my eyes can say, "Wow. These are amazing ideas we're learning, aren't they?"

"Repeating lines?"

"Comeback lines?"

"Which do you think?" They settled on the latter title.

Look over your chart again. This time think aloud with the children about how to fill it in.

"So, writers, let's chart your ideas. You said that Angela Johnson, in *Joshua's Night Whispers*, uses one phrase over and over."I held my marker pen over the box in column two. "What should we write here?"

The children made suggestions, and they were charted. "What should we write in this third column?" Soon the chart looked like this.

I like both of these options. They are both transparent.

I rephrase the idea that she repeats "night whispers" to make it more generic: She repeats a key phrase. This is a replicable technique.

Where?	What do you see?	Why is she doing this?	We call it . . .	Other Books?
Joshua's Night Whispers	3 dots, 3 times	Slows reader down, something more is going to happen	Dot, dot, dot.	*The Leaving Morning* **Our Stories**
Joshua's Night Whispers	One phrase, 5 times	They keep coming back and they hold the main idea of the story	Comeback lines	

This chart will thread through your entire unit. You'll want to be certain it is large enough for children to see. Many teachers devote a whole bulletin board to this chart.

Link

Remind children of the thinking they've done. Suggest children can search other Angela Johnson books for these craft elements, notice yet others, or use these in their own writing.

"As writers, we have learned so much from our mentor author. Not only have we been thinking about *what* she does but also *why* she does it. Let's be thoughtful writers and keep thinking like this. As you work today, you might want to study some of Angela Johnson's other books to see if you find 'dot, dot, dot' or comeback lines in those other books. Or you could try to notice *on your own* another technique she uses, and you could try to think about why she uses that technique."

When children study Joshua by the Sea; Mama Bird, Baby Birds; One of Three; *or* When I Am Old With You, *they'll again see ellipses and/or comeback lines! In* Rain Feet, *they'll also notice sound words such as "plop!" and "splash!"*

TIME TO CONFER

During this unit of study, many of your conferences will be with children as they read rather than as they write. You'll find that children tend to notice the *content* not the *craft* in a text. If a page contains the list of all the places Joshua walks (past the toy box, down the hall), the young reader will notice Joshua's pretty toy box but not notice the fact that the author has *listed* places Joshua travels. This shouldn't surprise you.

If you want to cultivate an awareness of the craftsmanship choices an author has made, one way to do this is to ask, "Why do you suppose she didn't write it like this?" and then give an alternative. Why didn't she just write, "I hear night noises so I go find daddy?" Why'd she include a long list of all the places he walked? Why didn't Angela call these night *noises* instead of night *whispers*?" See the conferences cited to the right.

Another way to help children become aware of an author's writing technique is to ask children to notice ways the author's writing style is similar across a few pages. For example, even the titles of *Joshua's Night Whispers* and *The Leaving Morning* have fascinating similarities. You could mark selected pages from different texts and ask children to really study them and to talk for as long as they can about the ways those few pages are similar to each other. You'll find children's observations quite wonderful. Don't worry if children are spending a little less time than usual actually writing in this writing workshop session. The close study of another author's craft is also valuable.

These conferences in *The Conferring Handbook* may be especially helpful today:

▶ *"You Can Use Ellipses to Show Waiting"*
▶ *"Use a Refrain"*
▶ *"I See You're Adding an Exclamation Mark to Your Story Like Mem Fox Does"*

Also, if you have *Conferring with Primary Writers*, you may want to refer to the following conference:

▶ *"But How Did You Feel in Your Story?"*

When we study an author we might think a[bout]

★ Where the ideas come from
★ How the books are alike or How the books are different

AFTER-THE-WORKSHOP SHARE

Read another of Angela Johnson's books aloud, and ask students to compare the writing techniques with those in *Joshua's Night Whispers*.

"Some of you spent time studying *The Leaving Morning*. You looked to see if Angela Johnson used words again and again as she did in *Joshua's Night Whispers*. Let's all think about this. I'm going to reread a bit of the story, and then let's hear what some of you found." I read half of the book.

"Let me stop there. What are you finding?"

"She says '*the leaving morning*.' She says it three times."

"That's the main thing in the story."

"The *night whispers*; they're sort of the same as *the leaving morning*."

Ask students to, in partnerships, compare the writing techniques in their own writing with those Angela uses.

"Writers, I love the way you are studying what Angela does and using those same techniques in your writing. Would you get with your partners now, and partner two, read your writing aloud? Partner one, will you listen just like you listened to *The Leaving Morning*? Notice whether your friend has used any strategies that Angela Johnson uses when she writes."

When you examine a text to notice the way in which it has been written, it's helpful if the text is a familiar one. You can study just a portion of the text and, in fact, it's often best to do so.

Of course there are many parallels between The Night Whispers *and* The Leaving Morning. *Neither phrase is a common one!*

For most of the children, the one way in which their writing will most obviously resemble Angela Johnson's is that they've added ellipses into their stories. A few children, however, will also have tried to incorporate comeback lines into their drafts. When Ramon pulled close to his partner and read aloud *Legos Soaring* [*Fig. V-1*], his partner counted the number of places he used Angela Johnson's strategies in his writing. The list was long!

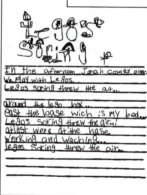

Fig. V-1   Ramon

Legos Soaring
In the afternoon Jonah
comes over. We play
with Legos. Legos
soaring through the
air . . . around the
Lego box . . . past the
base, which is my bed . . .
Legos soaring through
the air. . . . At last
we're at the house,
working and watching . . .
Legos soaring through
the air. . . .

LEARNING FROM ANGELA: WRITING COMEBACK LINES

GETTING READY

- Enlarged text of different comeback lines (or copy on an overhead a page from your notepad)
- Piece of writing (prewritten) on which you are working
- Note cards
- Craft chart
- Angela Johnson's books
- Sticky notes with your selected comeback line
- See CD-ROM for resources

IN THE PREVIOUS SESSION, STUDENTS NOTICED that Angela Johnson often uses a repeating phrase in her books, one that holds the central idea of the story. They named these phrases "comeback lines." In today's minilesson, you will show children how you sometimes do likewise in your writing, so that they can do likewise in theirs.

In this minilesson, you will help children understand your standards for measuring possible candidate phrases, and you will help them see that you weigh many possibilities before settling on one. You will also show them that it takes a bit of experimentation before you determine how and where to use this technique.

The real point of this lesson lies not in the successful use of comeback phrases but rather in the larger lesson you are teaching. When we admire a strategy another writer has used, we can then use that same strategy in our own writing. Moreover, as writers, we do not think only about what to say; we also think about how to say it.

In this session, you'll demonstrate how students can incorporate a special feature from another author's work into their own writing.

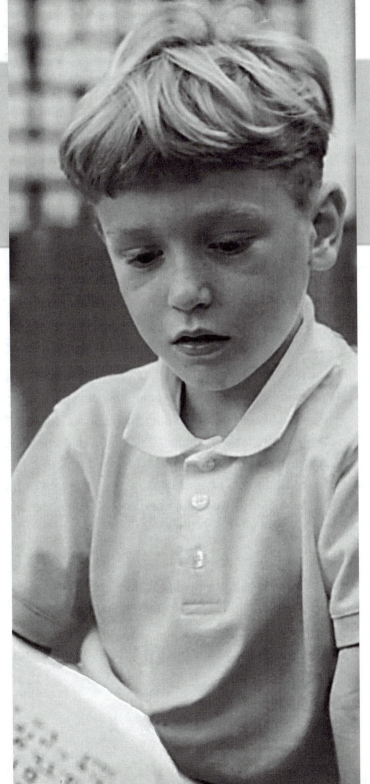

The Minilesson

Connection

Remind students of the strategy in Angela Johnson's writing that they admired in the previous session, and tell them that today you'll show them how to use that strategy in their writing.

"Yesterday we noticed that Angela Johnson uses what we called 'comeback lines' in her stories. The phrase 'night whispers' is not only part of the title in *Joshua's Night Whispers*, but the phrase is repeated four more times. We noticed the same with *The Leaving Morning*. Angela Johnson repeats the phrase 'the leaving morning' at least five times. Today I'm going to show you how you can use comeback lines in your own stories, too."

Teaching

Demonstrate and name the process you use to devise a comeback line for your writing.

"Let me show you how I found a comeback line for my rainy day story. Listen to what I did because later I am going to ask you to tell your partner the steps I went through. First, I needed to find a phrase that sounded right and carried the main idea of my story. So I reread my story, asking, 'Did I already use some words that could become my comeback line, my refrain?' Listen with me and see what you think." Amanda reread her story thoughtfully as if testing the words:

> The rain had just stopped.
> I was sitting on the cross-town bus, staring out the window, watching the sky turn pale blue.
> I saw people open their jackets. I saw puddles misting in the sun.
> Suddenly I looked up . . . all around me the buildings were sparkling.

Usually we begin our connection by saying, "Yesterday we . . ." and then describing prior work using a generalization. Then we zoom in and supply an emblematic detail which helps children recall the previous work. Finally we name our teaching point.

As Amanda read her draft aloud, she visibly paused after particular lines and showed that she weighed whether a portion of that line could become a refrain.

Over and over in these minilessons we demonstrate a step-by-step process that we hope children will follow. We reenact and role-play rather than talking about a process.

"I considered 'misting in the sun,' but it wouldn't be right to have misting at the beginning. I don't really see a line in my story that tells the true and honest way I feel about that winter day. So I will list possible lines on a separate piece of paper. I'm going to write about how that day made me feel." For a moment, Amanda tucked her head, jotting phrases on her clipboard. "Let me read my list:"

brightness all around
winter glory
winter smiles
a smile-making day
winter is smiling

"Now I am going to read over my list and think to myself, 'Which one of these will work in more than one place in my story?" Amanda was silent for a minute, reading. Then she said,"I pick 'winter smiles'" (and she wrote it on a sticky note). "Now, I'm going to move that phrase to different places to see where it might work. Listen and let me know if you think it works."

The rain had just stopped.
I was sitting on the cross-town bus, staring out the
window, watching the sky turn pale blue.

Amanda added Winter smiles, and stuck her note bearing these words onto this section of her text. The children nodded in approval.

I saw people open their jackets. I saw puddles misting in the sun.

Amanda added Winter smiles and children agreed it worked there, too.

Suddenly, I looked up . . . and all around me the buildings were sparkling.

Once again Amanda added Winter smiles into both the oral and written transcript.

The challenge is to make the mental gymnastics of writing into a concrete and simple process. Instead of mentally weighing her options, Amanda writes the refrain on a large sticky note and shows the children how she literally experiments with places where she could add this phrase. She makes an abstract process into a concrete one.

When Amanda jotted potential phrases onto her clipboard earlier in the minilesson, she could have actually pre-written at least the one phrase she uses, copying it onto a bunch of post-its. If she had pre-made several movable sticky notes containing the refrain, this would make this revision strategy much more accessible to children.

Reread your writing and think aloud, "What has this revision accomplished? How does it change my piece?"

Then Amanda reread the whole text, with the new comeback lines inserted throughout it.

The rain had just stopped.
I was sitting on the cross-town bus, staring out the window, watching the sky turn pale blue.
Winter smiles.
I saw people open their jackets. I saw puddles misting in the sun.
Winter smiles.
Suddenly I looked up . . . all around me the buildings were sparkling.
Winter smiles.

"What do you think?"

Max: "It makes it sound softer."

Stefanos: "You read it slower."

Amanda: "It kind of sounds like a poem."

Alina: "It would make a good title for your story, too."

"Thank you. I feel like my writing is all of a sudden good enough to put in a frame!"

Active Engagement

Ask partners to retell the steps you took.

"So, writers, would you get with your partner and retell the steps I've gone through to add a comeback line into my story, as we saw that Angela Johnson had done in her stories. Retell the steps across your fingers."

Link

Send students off to study Angela Johnson and to incorporate strategies they notice into their own writing.

"Today some of you might want to reread *The Leaving Morning* or *Joshua's Night Whispers* to notice again where and how Angela Johnson uses her comeback lines, or to notice other strategies she uses to make her writing

Remember that strategies must be used for purposes. Comeback lines aren't always assets to a piece of writing. It's important to help writers think, "What have I accomplished?"

Usually we suggest children try out (rather than talk about) a strategy, but in the interest of time, Amanda settled on this efficient form of active engagement.

beautiful. Others might want to try any of the techniques we've noticed (or others) in your own writing. If anyone wants to try comeback lines but is not sure how to get started, you can stay here on the rug with me."

MID-WORKSHOP TEACHING POINT

Show readers how to carefully use the techniques they are learning with an example from the class.

"I saw that a lot of us are trying out some of the strategies that we have been learning from Angela Johnson. One thing that I know is that we don't want to write our 'dot, dot, dots" just anywhere, and we don't want to choose just any old comeback line. You need to think, 'What's really important here? What do I want my readers to understand?" Let me share with you a piece Ron is working on. Here he is writing about a test he has to take. But he's decided he really wants his reader to know how scared he is. Writers can use "dot, dot, dot," comeback lines, or other strategies to bring out the big thing in our stories."

Amanda read the piece of writing. [*Fig. VI-1*]

"So guys, if any of you are using strategies you've learned from Angela Johnson, be sure you also ask, 'What's the big thing I'm trying to show?' Right now, before you do anything more, would you read the piece you are working on to your partner and tell your partner what the big thing is that you are trying to show."

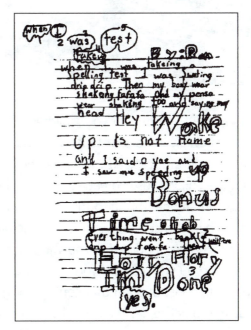

Fig. VI-1   Ron

When I was taking [the] test
By Ron

When I was taking a spelling test I was sweating: drip, drip. Then my body was shaking: fa fa fa. And my pen was shaking too and [I] said to my head, "Hey, wake up, it's not home." And I said, "Oh yeah." And I saw me speeding up.
"Bonus time."
"Oh-oh."
Everything went black, drip, drip, fa fa fa. Hurry, hurry!
I'm done.
Yes.

Time to Confer

Today's minilesson will fly right over your children's heads unless you come back to it in conferences. It's especially important to do so because you don't want the author study to end up as an ellipses study! Read the conferences cited at right and notice how Amanda helped the children use comeback lines in their writing. Notice not only the content of these conferences, but also the teaching method she uses (for example, demonstration). When you confer, try to follow the architecture of conferences and to remember that when you decide *what* you will teach in your conference, you will also need to decide *how* you will teach. If you are going to demonstrate, let the bold statements about demonstration in that conference guide your practice. If you are going to use guided practice, let those bold statements guide your practice.

This conference in *The Conferring Handbook* may be especially helpful today:
▶ *"Use a Refrain"*

Also, if you have *Conferring with Primary Writers*, you may want to refer to the following conference:
▶ *"Are You Stuck?"*

After-the-Workshop Share

Ask students to talk with their partners about anything new they might have tried that Angela does.

"In our writing workshop, some of you have been trying to use strategies Angela Johnson uses in her writing so you've used 'dot, dot, dot' and comeback lines in your stories. But I'm wondering if any of you have noticed other things Angela Johnson does in her writing, and if any of you have tried *those* things? Would you and your partner talk about whether you have done anything else that Angela Johnson does? Turn and talk." The children talked, and soon I called on a few to talk into the circle.

Ask a few students to share what they've tried.

"Jordan and I noticed that she tells what time it is. Like in *The Leaving Morning*, it is early in the morning. . . ."

"Because it is misty!"

"And the sweeper is sweeping. He comes when I am up early."

"What an interesting thing to notice! I can see what you mean that in *The Leaving Morning*, Angela tells the time of day. But does she do it in any other books?"

"Yeah, *Joshua's Night Whispers*."

"You're right! Wow!"

"So did you and Jordan try that in your writing? Are you giving your readers clues about what time of day it is in your stories?"

"Yeah, I'm telling about when I had a bad dream. I wrote, 'In the dark, dark night under the light of the moon, I woke up.'"

Use the students' ideas to add to the chart.

"You really do put us in the nighttime! Just like Angela Johnson. So we should definitely add that to our chart."I added to the chart.

Where?	What do you see?	Why is she doing this?	We call it...	Other Books?
Joshua's Night Whispers	3 dots, 3 times	Slows reader down, something more is going to happen	Dot, dot, dot.	*The Leaving Morning* Our Stories
Joshua's Night Whispers	One phrase, 5 times	They keep coming back and they hold the main idea of the story	Comeback lines	*The Leaving Morning* Our Stories
The Leaving Morning	Books start with time of day	Instead of starting with weather, starts with time	Time of day	*Joshua's Night Whispers*

IF CHILDREN NEED MORE TIME

- Plan a strategy lesson in which you invite those interested in trying to use comeback lines to stay with you on the rug. This will not only provide support, it will get more children to actually try this in their own writing.

- You can do a minilesson where you have the students try this technique with a shared writing piece that the class has made together. Remember to first ask, "What do we want to really show in our story?"

- Find children's books that have comeback lines and read these aloud as if you hadn't realized. Your children will love to be the ones to point out to you that the author has used a comeback line. Books to use include:

Mem Fox	*Time for Bed*
Cynthia Rylant	*When I Was Young in the Mountains*
Paul Showers	*The Listening Walk*
Audrey Wood	*The Napping House*
Charlotte Zolotow	*I Like to Be Little*

Be prepared to enjoy children's approximations as they try incorporating Angela Johnson's techniques into their own writing. Don't be surprised to see anything you've taught being overused, and don't worry when you see children floundering. Remember when you first put on roller skates, or first played an instrument, or first tried to ski. Your children will be learning to do something new, and all of us learn to do new things through approximation.

You may find it helpful to separate your children's efforts to make reading-writing connections into categories. Is there a group of children who thinks that learning from this mentor author means writing about the *topics* in Angela Johnson's books rather than her craftsmanship? It shouldn't surprise you if some children keep focusing on *what* texts say rather than on the author's craft. This is age-appropriate behavior. Is there a group of children who thinks that reading-writing connections are made simply by sprinkling ellipses randomly through writing drafts? If you see such things, be slow to conclude that the children have no logic behind what they are doing. Ask these children to explain why they did this or used other strategies.

Are there some children who are making deliberate decisions about what techniques will and will not serve their purposes? How will you make these children and their work famous in your community?

Are there children who imitate their own reading-writing corrections, and do so involving authors other than your mentor author? These children can become teachers during upcoming sessions.

STUDYING ANGELA'S WRITING, THEN LEARNING FROM IT: USING RESEARCH DETAILS

GETTING READY

▶ *Make Way for Ducklings* (you will have read this to the class prior to this session)
▶ *The Leaving Morning*
▶ Piece of shared writing (class will have written this together previously)
▶ Revision pens and paper, tape
● See CD-ROM for resources

SO FAR IN THIS UNIT OF STUDY, YOU'VE ASKED CHILDREN *to look at texts written by Angela Johnson and to notice features of the writing that they like. The children noticed ellipses and repeating lines.*

Sometimes, when your kids are studying the texts another author has written, you'll decide that regardless of what your students notice in an author's writing, there are some aspects of writing that you want to highlight.

In this session, you'll ask children to notice the detailed specific information in Angela Johnson's book. In this particular minilesson, you'll finesse this by telling the children that in the previous session, a few of them noticed that The Leaving Morning *contained a lot of facts. You'll act as if this minilesson grew out of that observation.*

In this session, you'll show children that Angela Johnson writes with precise detail and suggest that she gathered this detail from research. Then you'll invite the class to do likewise, both in a piece of shared writing and in the writing they do in their own lives.

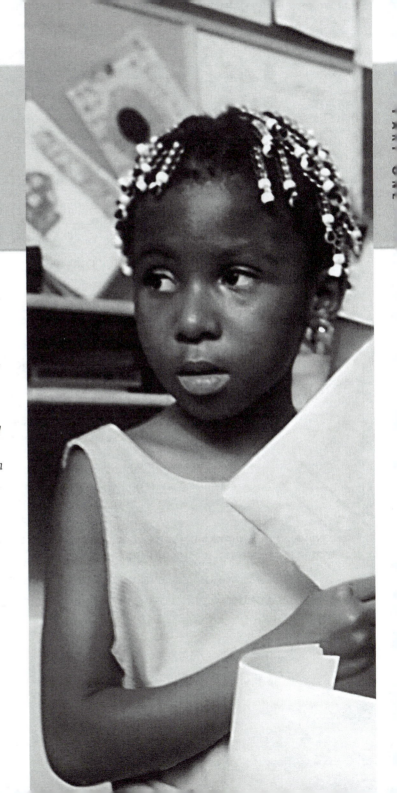

The Minilesson

Connection

Remind children that they have already noticed that Angela uses small bits of real information in her writing.

"Yesterday, a few of you told me that you noticed that in *The Leaving Morning*, Angela Johnson added 'lots of facts.' I was thinking about that last night and I realized you were onto something important. She *could* have written this."

> The other day we moved.
> I kissed the window good-bye.
> Then we moved.

"But instead, like you said, her story has a lot of information in it."

> It was the leaving morning. Boxes of clothes, toys, dishes, and pictures of us everywhere. . . . We woke up early and had hot cocoa from the deli across the street. I made more lips on the deli window and watched for the movers on the leaving morning. . . . We sat on the steps and watched the movers. They had blue moving clothes on and made bumping noises on the stairs. There were lots of whistles and "Watch out, kids."

Teach children that these small bits of information come from a writer's senses, from research into the subject of the writing.

"Today, we can all learn from Angela Johnson that when writers write, we get some of our information from our minds, and we also get some of our information from doing research."

I highlight the importance of a particular technique by showing what the text might have looked like without the benefit of the technique. By juxtaposing two versions (one with and one without a technique), I hope to drive home the value of the technique.

This is a nice clear teaching point. Notice that I tell children we are learning something that writers use often.

Teaching

Tell children that for McCloskey to write his book, he kept ducks in his bathtub and researched them.

"Do you know the book, *Make Way for Ducklings*? Robert McCloskey wrote that book about something that happened one day long ago—in a busy city, he saw ducks walk across the street. All the traffic stopped for them. To write about ducks, though, Robert McCloskey had to do research. He wanted to really know how ducks walk and quack—so he got two ducks and kept them in his New York City apartment, and sometimes, when he was writing his story, he put his pen down and went over to his ducks to just watch them so he would have the exact words to describe them."

Speculate that Angela, too, may have done some research to write her books.

"We don't know exactly what Angela Johnson did to write *The Leaving Morning*, but she *may* have driven back to her old block just to see if seeing it could spark memories—like the memory of the diner across the street. She *may* have watched movers at someone else's house and noticed their blue moving clothes and their whistles. Or she may have talked to people about their moving day. What we *do* know is that a writer like Angela Johnson or Robert McCloskey often gets his or her details by doing research!"

Active Engagement

Revisit a piece of writing the children have done together as a class and help the children use firsthand research to add details.

"Let's look at the piece we wrote in science the other day. Remember we wrote, 'It was science time. We went to look at our frog eggs. We couldn't believe our eyes. We saw tadpoles!' Let's look again at our tank—let's research—and see if that gives us something to add to our piece."

Jordan said, "They look like small little black dots spinning around."

"Wow, what a neat way to talk about the tadpoles, they are like black little dots spinning and swimming around. That would make a great addition to our piece. What do you guys think?"

"And tell that we were talking and pointing 'cause we are."

Remember that planning a minilesson involves a kind of writing. This minilesson profits from the same qualities that make for good writing. The details (and the anecdote) about McCloskey draw listeners into the minilesson just as details and anecdotes draw readers into other written texts.

When I plan for the teaching component of a minilesson, I think not only "What will I teach?" but also "How will I teach?" One method that I use in both minilessons and conferences is "explain and give an example." The challenge when using this method is to explain in ways that are interesting and memorable. I sometimes tell teachers that this method involves giving a tiny keynote speech. In this minilesson, my teaching method is "explain and give an example" and I make my explanation memorable by telling an anecdote.

Show children the two versions of the story—the original and the one with the research details added. Talk over the differences.

Original Story	New Version
It was science time. We went to look at our frog eggs. We couldn't believe our eyes. We saw tadpoles.	It was science time. We went to look at our frog eggs. Everyone was talking and pointing at the tank. We couldn't believe our eyes. We saw our tadpoles swimming. We saw little black dots spinning and swimming around!

Again, it helps to juxtapose before and after versions.

"Writers, would you and your partner do more research (observe them some more) and see if you have more information you could add to our piece?" As students began to talk, they came up with lots of different details to add on to the piece.

It was science time.
We went to look at our frog eggs.
Everyone was talking and pointing at the tank.
We couldn't believe our eyes.
We saw little black dots spinning and swimming around!
Our tadpoles were wiggling around the tank in a panic.
They bumped against the tank as if they were saying, "Let me out! Let me out!"

In this bit of active involvement, children use the shared text as a place to practice the strategy I've taught. Whenever I ask students to work on a shared story, I try to make sure the story grows out of our classroom life together. I don't want to ask them to add onto a story about my sons!

Link

Ask children to do some research for their own writing. If they can't do the research in school, they can visualize their subjects to research them.

"So writers, let's add 'researches for details' to our chart of what we notice—maybe some of you can stay after the minilesson and help me fill it out."

Where?	What do you see?	Why is she doing this?	We call it . . .	Other Books?
Joshua's Night Whispers	3 dots, 3 times	Slows reader down, something more is going to happen	Dot, dot, dot.	*The Leaving Morning* *Our Stories*
Joshua's Night Whispers	One phrase, 5 times	They keep coming back and they hold the main idea of the story	Comeback lines	*The Leaving Morning* *Our Stories*
The Leaving Morning	Books start with time of day	Instead of starting with weather, starts with time	Time of day	*Joshua's Night Whispers*
The Leaving Morning	Lots of facts, details	Helps us picture what happened	Researches for details	*Make Way for Ducklings*

"Now you all have even more choices for what you'll do today. How many of you are starting new stories and writing them with some of these things—comeback lines, researched details—in mind? Thumbs up." A dozen children signaled that this was their plan. "How many of you will be revising and might try some research today, or add comeback lines?"

"Great. I know it'll be hard to do research *in* school if you are writing something that happened *out* of school, but remember, you can reread your stories and pretend to be in the place you describe. Sometimes you can remember more information to add to your story. And don't forget that you can use your revision tools, like the purple revision pens or the revision paper and tape, to do this."

Remember that any one day's minilesson should add to your children's repertoire of strategies. Try to avoid regularly teaching minilessons that then become that day's assigned work. Writing requires us to draw on all that we know, but mostly to follow our content and language where they lead.

TIME TO CONFER

Today's minilesson paves the way for lots of wonderful conferences. You'll probably say phrases like these:

▶ "What I do is I reread and think, 'Which part is especially important?' Can you do that? Oh! I'm glad you chose that part. So if you were going to research something that would help you add to this page (like we researched the fish tank), what might you study? So let's do that together." Perhaps, also, "So let's pretend it's right here in front of us. What do you see?"

▶ "Sometimes I pretend I'm doing the thing and then I say, 'Wait. Let me write it down, step by step. Let's do that. Pretend you are acting out the story."

▶ "Let's pretend you were doing that right now. Show me how it went. What did you do first—show me. Oh! So does your story start, 'One day, I was walking along and then I slipped and fell on my knee?'" The child nods. "Say that then."

▶ "Can you picture it? Get that time in your mind. What happens first? How did it start?"

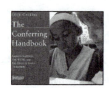

These conferences in *the Conferring Handbook* may be especially helpful today:

▶ *"You Can Use Ellipses to Show Waiting"*
▶ *"Use a Refrain"*
▶ *"I See You're Adding an Exclamation Mark to Your Story Like Mem Fox Does"*

Also, if you have *Conferring with Primary Writers*, you may want to refer to the following conferences:

▶ "Are You Sure You Are Done Writing?"
▶ "Can We Study What This Author Did and Let Her Teach Us Some Lessons?"

Find a child who has tried to add research details to his work the way Angela Johnson does. Tell the class the story of that child's process.

"Jamal has been working on a piece about when his coat was stuck in the closet door. Today, he'd already written, 'I went to get my coat. We were going to the yard. My coat was stuck in the closet! I pulled it and pulled it and it popped out.' He decided that he wanted to be like Angela Johnson and do some research to help him add more to his story. He went over to the closet and looked at it really hard, paying attention to every little detail. He even tried opening and closing it, and when he did, he remembered that his coat was stuck in the crack of space where the door bends. He went back and added, 'My coat was stuck in the crack of the closet door. It was pinching on my sleeve.'"

If a child has tried writing in other ways like Angela Johnson, you might tell the story of that child's process as well.

"Samantha did the coolest thing today, guys. She'd been working on a piece about all the things she loves to see in the night sky when she looks up at it. We got to talking about how her writing was kind of like Angela Johnson's, and maybe she could get some more ideas about how to make her writing stronger by looking at Angela's books. We remembered how Angela likes to use those comeback phrases, like 'the leaving morning.' What idea did you get from Angela to try in your story, Sam?"

"I made my comeback phrase. Because in my story I keep on looking up and seeing different stuff, so I put 'When I looked up' again and again because that's the most important part."

"Writers, we can learn from Jamal and from Samantha!"

Stories have great teaching power. It's wise to tell stories of your children's writing processes.

It is more effective to reenact using a strategy than it is to simply show the results of using that strategy. Here, I give a blow-by-blow retelling of how two children ended up writing like Angela. This is more effective instruction than simply showing the products.

Post-Workshop Teaching Point

Ask children to do the same work tonight at home that they did today during writing workshop.

"Tonight when you go home, would you remember that writers do research, just like Robert McCloskey did in *Make Way for Ducklings* and like Angela Johnson did in *The Leaving Morning* and like Jamal did today for his 'coat stuck in the closet' story."

Tell children to conduct some research to add details to their writing. Give examples.

"You can interview someone or look at photographs or even go back to where your story took place to spark your memory and to gather more information for revising your stories."

"For example, Isabelle told me that she is going ice skating tonight, so she is going to do some research to see if she notices any details that might be important information to add to her ice skating story. And Daniel is going to look at some photographs of himself on the parallel bars during his gymnastics meet."

Ask children to share their plans aloud.

"Turn and tell your partner the research *you* will be doing this afternoon when you get home."

Remind children of the research they will do tonight and always.

"This afternoon and tonight and for the rest of your lives, don't forget to be researchers. Come back tomorrow, ready to add some new information to your stories."

When listing authors, try to include a published author or two plus a child from your own class.

It is important for children to learn that writers live more attentive lives because they are writing.

Again, details help our minilessons just like they help any piece of writing. These specific examples of the way two children plan to research their topics can show children what you hope they'll do.

Notice that we use the structure of minilessons for most of our teaching. Can you find the connection? The link?

▶ There are very few qualities of good writing that matter more than details. Tell the class how another published author researched his or her story. "To write *Fireflies*, Julie Brinkloe probably went back to her memories of catching fireflies, and remembered the whooping kids and the blinking lights of the fireflies. You can research your stories also. Picture what you are writing about in your minds (or look at a photograph or ask someone who was there)."

▶ Share how you researched your story. "I wanted to say more about singing in our church choir so the next time I was in the choir, I paid a lot of attention. I noticed our choir robes, and the way the organ music made me feel."

▶ Teach writers to go back to the place of the story and observe, bringing a clipboard.

▶ Teach writers to decide on one page that matters the most, and to draw a detailed picture of that part of the incident. The drawing can help us remember details.

STUDYING ONE TEXT FOR MANY LESSONS

GETTING READY

▶ Blank copy of the Craft chart
▶ A system for dividing your children into small groups (see the connection phase of the minilesson)
▶ A typed transcript of *Joshua's Night Whispers* for each student
▶ A copy of the transcript of *Joshua's Night Whispers* placed onto chart paper on your easel
⬤ See CD-ROM for resources

FOR THE PAST FEW DAYS, YOU HAVE HELPED THE WHOLE CLASS *find sections they admire in* Joshua's Night Whispers, *speculate why Angela Johnson used a particular craft technique, and then find other instances where she (or other authors) used that technique. Finally, you have encouraged children to try the same techniques in their own writing. By now, if your children are first or second graders, they should be able to continue doing this with less support from you. Without your presence, they'll no doubt probe less, but you can hope they'll do their six- and seven-year-old best.*

Today you'll invite your children to continue filling in the Craft chart with less support from you. (Bypass this minilesson if you teach kindergarteners, or invent a way to bring this content to your children.)

Before approaching this session, you'd benefit from trying your own hand at this. What could you imagine admiring in Joshua's Night Whispers? *Do you love the way Angela Johnson stretches out Joshua's walk so that readers can see each bit of it? If I were writing about waking up and wanted to emulate her example, I'd first stir in my bed, then open one eye, then sit up and yawn. You may love the way night whispers are at the start of the story, the middle, then the end. If I were writing about my cat, maybe she'd meow often in my book. Maybe you admire the big change: Joshua is alone and uneasy at first and safe with his father at the end. Maybe you admire that an object—the rabbit—threads its way through the whole story. Of course, the challenge for you is to not only admire the craftsmanship of Angela Johnson's story but to do what you hope your students will do and emulate what you admire!*

THE MINILESSON

Connection

Set up and streamline a system for forming small groups during the minilesson.

"Writers, before we start the minilesson, we're going to combine partnerships into groups of four today. So the partners sitting beside each other in the first row, would you connect with the partners right behind you? Would partnerships sitting together in the third row connect with partners in the fourth row behind you? Touch hands so I can see you've formed groups of four. Okay. Turn back towards me, guys. Okay, we'll call these 'groups,' not 'partners.' Let's practice getting into *groups*. In a minute, I'll say *groups* and when I say this, then you'll turn to your group." I paused. "Okay, *groups* please. Do it quickly so we don't waste one precious minute of writing time." Students turned to form groups. "Writers, that was nice. You can face me again. We'll be using these groups for the next few days."

I try to get logistics like these out of the way so they don't overwhelm the content I am trying to teach. Once I create a system for dividing into groups, I'll use that system with consistency whenever I want children to form small groups.

Tell writers they'll be filling out the author-observation chart on their own.

"Writers, do you remember when you learned to ride your bike? Probably many of you had training wheels at first. After riding with training wheels for a while, the training wheels got taken off and you rode on your own."

"In the last few days when we've been looking at Angela Johnson's book and filling out our chart with what we noticed, I've been right here helping you do every step of the way—sort of like I'm your training wheels. Today I want to take off the training wheels. I'm not going to help you."

"For the past few days, we have studied Angela Johnson's craft and we have charted what we noticed. Today we are going to look again at *Joshua's Night Whispers* and see if we can notice something else Angela does in her writing."

I tell children that so far they've had a lot of help from me—training wheels—and that today they'll begin to carry on more independently because I'm trying to rally them for the challenge that lies ahead.

The reason we keep returning to Joshua's Night Whispers *(not* The Leaving Morning*) is that by now, each child in the class can read* Joshua's Night Whispers. *If your children can all read* The Leaving Morning, *use that as your exemplar.*

Generalize the purpose of today's minilesson so you are not just assigning today's work but also teaching towards tomorrow.

"Writers do this. We learn a zillion lessons from one example because we really, really study it closely, and we learn to study books on our own. This way, any book we love can become our teacher."

Teaching and Active Engagement

Read an excerpt aloud and ask children to work in groups to fill in charts about the techniques Angela Johnson has used.

"This time, I'm going to read the first part of Angela Johnson's story aloud twice, and I want you to listen and to think about what she is doing. Then you are going to talk in groups about a technique Angela is using that you haven't noticed before. You'll need to talk about each of the columns on our chart."

By revisiting the same small, simple text over and over, we teach kids to look closely and to see more than that which first meets the eye. If we continually move on to new, exotic texts, children will point at that which is most obvious, and they will be less likely to let the text nudge them to invent a new idea about good writing.

"Before I start, notice the book I'm going to read. You should be able to fill out your first column before I go any further." Then I read the first seven lines (three pages) from *Joshua's Night Whispers*. "I'm going to stop right there. Remember you are going to talk about. . . ." I read the titles from each column in the chart. "Let me reread one last time and you think about this second column, 'What do you see?'"

Again, I read the first seven lines of the book. "Okay, groups, turn and talk." And as children turned to form groups, I passed one typed copy of the text to each group.

I time my final reading so that I have already given all the directions and directed kids to listen with attention to the second column in their chart. Then I get them off to a good start by rereading the passage one last time.

The instructions to "turn and talk" are familiar ones to these children, but until now, they've responded by talking to their partner. This time, they talk with their group. The single page provides a central focus for each of the groups.

"So, I'm passing a clipboard with a chart on it to each group, and you'll have a longer time on the carpet than usual—ten minutes—to see if you can find something you like and fill out the chart. Stay here on the rug—and get started."

When the minilesson is going to be longer than usual, it's wise to say so to kids. Children develop an internalized sense for the time frames of a minilesson.

Where?	What do you see?	Why is she doing this?	We call it . . .	Other Books?
Joshua's Night Whispers	3 dots, 3 times	Slows reader down, something more is going to happen	Dot, dot, dot.	*The Leaving Morning* *Our Stories*
Joshua's Night Whispers	One phrase, 5 times	They keep coming back and they hold the main idea of the story	Comeback lines	*The Leaving Morning* *Our Stories*
The Leaving Morning	Books start with time of day	Instead of starting with weather, starts with time	Time of day	*Joshua's Night Whispers*
The Leaving Morning	Lots of facts, details	Helps us picture what happened	Researches for details	*Make Way for Ducklings*
Joshua's Night Whispers				

Convene the class and solicit an observation.

Eventually I reconvened the class. "What do you see?" I asked.

"She lists."

"Can you show us?" I pointed to the chart-sized version of the book's text, which I had on my easel. Emma came up and pointed to the phrase, "past my toy box . . . and out my door . . . then down the hall."

Once a child has noticed something Angela Johnson does, recruit all the children to help you think about why the author does this.

"So let's look at this list." I looked at the list, modeling looking. I paused. I let time go by. "Why is she doing this?"

"It tells where he goes."

"It's all the same. 'Past my toy box' goes with 'out my door' goes with 'down the hall.'" Eric's intonation suggested that he was trying to say that there is a rhythm in the three phrases.

Again, the one shared copy brings children's attention to the same place.

I try not to convey by my intonation that I know the right answer and am quizzing children to see if they can guess. Instead, I ask why Angela has used a list as if I haven't yet pulled my observations together. I muse, right alongside the children.

"Oh! You are right! She makes everything in the list match." I reread the relevant excerpt to highlight this. "So would Angela write, 'I heard a growl that wasn't loud, a small whine and the dog makes a loud bark'?" I dictated this in a way that suggested it would have been discordant. "I don't think so. I think she'd say, 'I heard a quiet growl, a small whine, and a loud bark' so it matched. Not 'I heard a growl that wasn't loud, a small whine and the dog makes a loud bark.'"

Link

Encourage writers to find other instances of whatever they've noticed—and to use this or other strategies in their own writing.

"Today, before you get going on your writing, some of you might take a closer look at *The Leaving Morning* and see if she includes lists in that book as well. Or you may notice other things she does in *Joshua's Night Whispers* and look to see if whatever you notice is in both books. Others of you will get started right away, trying some of what you put on your chart in your own writing today. Let me know how it goes."

Drive home the idea that the elements in a list match each other by providing a contrary example, one in which the elements don't match. This concept is probably too advanced for most of the children but minilessons need to nudge even strong writers farther.

Angela Johnson does include lists in The Leaving Morning, as well as in Joshua's Night Whispers.

Where?	What do you see?	Why is she doing this?	We call it . . .	Other Books?
Joshua's Night Whispers	3 dots, 3 times	Slows reader down, something more is going to happen	Dot, dot, dot.	*The Leaving Morning* *Our Stories*
Joshua's Night Whispers	One phrase, 5 times	They keep coming back and they hold the main idea of the story	Comeback lines	*The Leaving Morning* *Our Stories*
The Leaving Morning	Books start with time of day	Instead of starting with weather, starts with time	Time of day	*Joshua's Night Whispers*
The Leaving Morning	Lots of facts, details	Helps us picture what happened	Researches for details	*Make Way for Ducklings*
Joshua's Night Whispers	She lists	So that there is a rhythm to the text	List of things	

MID-WORKSHOP TEACHING POINT

Intervene to remind kids that they need to make sure their work is readable. Ask kids to reread and check their writing with their partners.

"Guys, may I interrupt for a minute? I'm really pleased to see that many of you are using lots of techniques you've learned from Angela Johnson. But I want to remind you that sometimes when we revise, we aren't adding a nice new thing to our writing. Sometimes we revise because we reread our writing and say, 'Huh? I got to fix this.' Sometimes when we write, we skip words or forget punctuation. Sometimes when we try to reread what we have written, it doesn't sound right or make sense. Would you get with your partners before you go any further? Partner one, would you read your piece aloud and as you do so, partner two will you look at partner one's writing? When you find a place to make the writing more clear, make the changes if they're small ones or put a sticky note in that spot to tell you to do that tomorrow."

When we teach one thing, it's almost inevitable that other things fall by the wayside. Some of our interventions will extend the main direction of a unit, and others, like this one, will serve as corrections.

TIME TO CONFER

As you confer, it will be important for you to keep your eye on what matters most and to be willing to let go of what doesn't matter. For example, it matters that children look at the work of another author and come to their own observations about what that author has done and why. You can't expect children will come up with observations or insights as astute as those that you'd make! Be willing to let children do their five- and six-year-old best. Just as children need to approximate when they spell, they also need to approximate when they study the craftsmanship in a book. Read the conferences cited at right.

Then, too, it matters that your children look at their own writing and think not only about *what* they will say but also about *how* they will write. It matters that they deliberately use techniques they've admired in the work of other authors, that they try to use interesting techniques as they write, that they reread their own writing listening for the sounds of their language. If they do all this and yet add only ellipses (and overuse even those!), don't be discouraged.

Even when children are only approximating, you can see what they've done that is very smart indeed and name it for them. Try, also, to think of just one step forward a child might make, and to teach just that. The pattern in your conferences will be to research, to give a compliment, to make a suggestion, and then to send the child off with a reminder of how the child can use that suggestion not just today and in this piece, but also tomorrow and in future pieces.

These conferences in *The Conferring Handbook* may be especially helpful today:

▶ *"You Can Use Ellipses to Show Waiting"*
▶ *"Use a Refrain"*

Also, if you have *Conferring with Primary Writers*, you may want to refer to the following conferences:

▶ "Are You Stuck?"
▶ "As a Reader, I'd Love to Hear More About That"

AFTER-THE-WORKSHOP SHARE

Support the children's earlier work of adding research details to their writing. Tell the story of one child who has successfully added research details.

"When I was talking to Wei today he told me something so exciting about how he's been living like a writer and learning from Angela Johnson. He's been working on his piece about the construction happening on the sidewalk near his house. Yesterday, when he was walking home with his mom, he saw the workers and he remembered his piece. He did research like Angela Johnson might do, and looked *really hard* to notice every little detail so he could add to his piece today." "What did you add, Wei?"

"I put in the way the ground shakes up when they do the jackhammer!"

"You added a detail from what you noticed that day? What an accomplishment to add what you notice about your topic into your writing the way Angela does!"

You might tell the story of another child's process if the children seem to need more examples.

"Remember the other day when I asked you all to be researchers when you went home? Isabelle went ice skating and she did some research for her ice skating story. What research did you do?"

"Well, when I went on the ice, I noticed it was bumpy and that reminded me that that's why I fell. I tripped over a chunk of ice."

"I'm glad you explained *why* you fell. That's really good information. Did you add that to your story?"

"Yep. I added the bumpy ice part on this paper and I taped it in to my story. Now it makes more sense."

"Good for you, Isabelle. Your research helped you notice something that was missing in your story. That's what we are all trying to do."

I want to be certain that this unit of study teaches children to live like writers, paying attention to the details of their lives. Therefore, I return to this theme often.

Wei explains that he paid attention to the ground. I support this by naming what he has done that is exportable to other pieces and other days. Try to do this often.

Again, I rename what Isabelle has just done and do so in a way that makes her work universal.

IF CHILDREN NEED MORE TIME

You'll want to observe how this session went and decide how much time you want to invest in helping your children become more independent at studying texts, noticing craft techniques, charting what they see, and then emulating these strategies. Clearly the goal merits your teaching time! If you decide to stretch out this aspect of your unit, you might try the following strategies.

▶ Retell the story of a few children who came to their own conclusions about Angela Johnson's craft and charted what they noticed.

▶ Read aloud a new Angela Johnson text and ask children to make observations about how she wrote that text. You might draw their attention to a particular page and highlight her method for writing that page by showing what the page could have been like.

ASSESSMENT

You'll probably want to take your children's writing home and reread their pieces with a variety of lenses. One lens will be that of story language. You'll no doubt notice that some children are writing either in list-like sentences ("We went to McDonalds. I got a hamburger. I got a toy. I played with my toy. I said, 'Good.'"), or they are using social language within their written texts ("My mom came to school. I love my mommy. She is nice. I love her a lot. A LOT. She loves me too."). Most others, however, are probably trying story language. Sometimes, the effort to write in story language leads children to make mistakes that are not unlike those they make when they use invented spelling to tackle long, complex words. These errors show growth, and you need to celebrate that the child is reaching towards literary language even if this causes new errors. [*Fig. VIII-1*]

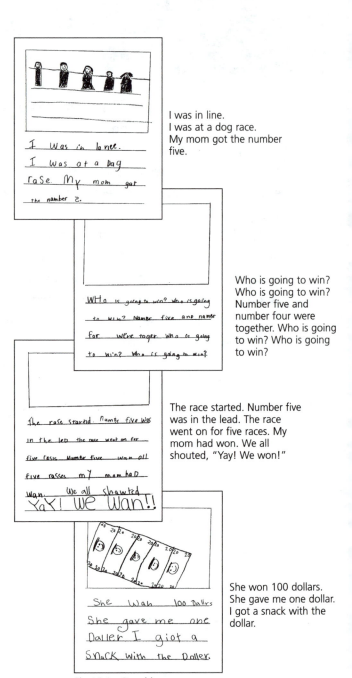

I was in line.
I was at a dog race.
My mom got the number five.

Who is going to win? Who is going to win? Number five and number four were together. Who is going to win? Who is going to win?

The race started. Number five was in the lead. The race went on for five races. My mom had won. We all shouted, "Yay! We won!"

She won 100 dollars. She gave me one dollar. I got a snack with the dollar.

Fig. VI-1   Ronald

NOTICING A NEW TEXT STRUCTURE: A MANY MOMENTS STORY

GETTING READY

▶ *Do Like Kyla*
▶ Student writing folders (with their pieces)
▶ *Alexander and the Terrible, Horrible, No Good, Very Bad Day* by Judith Viorst
▶ *Joshua by the Sea*
◯ See CD-ROM for resources

SO FAR IN THIS UNIT, YOUR STUDENTS *have used Angela Johnson's examples to learn strategies for improving their stories of one small moment. Today your author study enters part two. You will now emphasize that writers don't write only the story of one small moment, they write in other structures, sometimes writing texts that are a collection of many small moments. Angela Johnson's book, Do Like Kyla, is a series of episodes in which the younger sister tells what her older sister does and then says, "I do like Kyla." The book ends when, for once, the older sister emulates the younger one. The story is structured like beads on a string—concise, Small Moment vignettes held together by the repeating refrain of "I do like Kyla." The book is also held together by the larger story of the younger child following in her sister's footsteps across one entire day, until finally her big sister emulates the younger narrator.*

This session will describes Do Like Kyla as a "Many Moments" book, in contrast to the "Small Moment" books the children have been writing. It will let children know that writers need to decide—"Will I write about one small moment or about many moments linked together?"

In this session, you will read Do Like Kyla and let children study its Many Moments structure. You will get them started thinking about how to structure a story like this one.

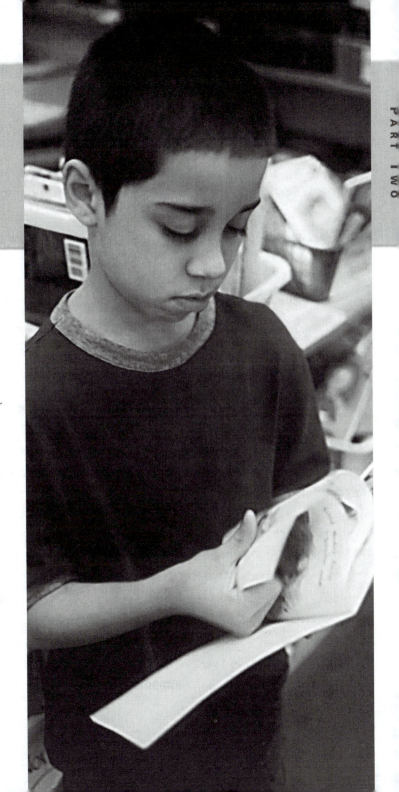

THE MINILESSON

Connection

Tell your children that all good books are not necessarily the story of one small moment. Read *Do Like Kyla* and ask, "Is this the story of one small moment?"

"Writers, you have gotten very skilled at taking a small moment and writing it as a story. Today I want us to read another Angela Johnson book and I want us to think about whether it is a story of one small moment or whether it is another kind of story. In this book, Angela writes about two girls who are sisters. The younger sister is the storyteller and she copies everything her big sister does, all day long." I read aloud *Do Like Kyla.* "So what do you think? Is this a Small Moment story? Talk in partners."

I convened the group. "What did you decide? Is this a Small Moment story?"

"No—cause it tells a lot of things."

"She kisses her dog and I kiss my cat sometimes."

"It starts with waking up and goes all day."

"It's like a list."

Tell students that authors sometimes decide to write a Many Moments story and give an example from your writing.

"What I want you to realize, writers, is that sometimes an author decides to make a piece that is like a necklace containing many small moments. As a writer, you get to choose—one small moment or a string of many moments."

"I could write the story of the moment when I got my new puppy. I held her in my arms and walked her into our house. That would be a one-moment story. *Or* I could write about *all* the times I've been glad to have a dog, telling one good time with my dog, then the next good time with her, and then the next good time."

"*Do Like Kyla* is a Many Moments story. For the next few days, let's study how to write a Many Moments piece."

Today's minilesson marks an important turning point. I'm moving the class from writing Small Moment stories towards writing texts that are structured in other ways. I use Do Like Kyla. *This book tells the story of a younger sister who imitates her older sister from morning to night; the book ends with the older sister imitating the younger one.*

We've called the stories children have been writing Small Moment stories; this text can be called a Many Moments story (rather like Viorst's Alexander and the No Good, Horrible, Very Bad Day).

Although I'm not emphasizing this now, in my example of a Many Moments story, all the moments are linked by the common focus of "good times with my dog." This distinguishes the Many Moments story from the unfocused retellings that we're avoiding.

Teaching

Reread part of *Do Like Kyla* and ask your students to notice what Angela Johnson has done.

"I want you to listen again to *Do Like Kyla*, just the first part of it. Listen and tell me what you notice Angela Johnson does as a writer." I read a section of *Do Like Kyla*.

"What do you notice?"

"She's a copycat." Tom referred to the younger sister in the book.

"She has a comeback line, 'just like Kyla.'"

"She repeats things."

"Each page is about copying her sister."

"She loves her sister. You can tell and stuff."

"They talk to each other—dialogue."

"So Angela writes Small Moment stories like *Joshua's Night Whispers* but *she also* writes books like *Do Like Kyla*. *Do Like Kyla* contains many moments. I wonder if any writers in this room might decide to write both ways!"

Active Engagement

Ask students to listen to another story and to tell their partner whether it's a Small-Moment or a Many Moments story. Read a bit of Viorst's *Alexander and the Terrible, Horrible, No Good, Very Bad Day*.

"So writers, I'm going to read you a little bit of a book and would you think, 'Is this a Small Moment story or is it a Many Moments story?' After I read a bit, I'm going to ask you to tell your partner what it is, and how you know. Listen." From the beginning of the book, I read one long sentence about how Alexander wakes up to find gum in his hair and stumbles out of bed only to get his clothes wet as he's brushing his teeth. I finished by reading:

> At breakfast Anthony found a Corvette Sting Ray car kit in his breakfast cereal box . . . but in my breakfast cereal box all I found was breakfast cereal.
> In the car pool Mrs. Gibson let Becky have a seat by the window. Audrey and Elliot got seats by the window too. I said I was being scrunched. . . .
> I could tell it was going to be a terrible, horrible, no good, very bad day.

For now, I let this list accumulate. I could make a big deal about any of these observations, but I want children to become accustomed to brainstorming observations about texts.

Children tend to see the very things you have taught them to see. You'll hear your own words coming back to you.

Cynthia Rylant's When I Was Young in the Mountains *is another example of a Many Moments piece. When we want to help children think about the structure of a text, it can be helpful to set several alongside each other. They are not about the same topic, but they are structured similarly.*

"Which kind of piece is it: a Small Moment piece or a Many Moments piece? Turn and tell your partner." The class agreed it's a Many Moments piece.

Link

Send students off to continue writing with Angela Johnson as a mentor, using either her craft techniques or her text structures. Ask students to tell their partner their plans for the day.

"You have lots of choices as writers today. You can write a new piece or revise ones you've already written. If you are revising, you may want to use *any* strategy you see Angela Johnson using. Turn and tell your partner your plan for writing today."

"I know that some people said that they were going to keep on revising. Others said that they were going to try writing in a Many Moments way like Angela Johnson did in *Do Like Kyla*. Be ready at the end of writing to share what you worked on."

TIME TO CONFER

Every unit of study contains a few crucial minilessons that represent turning points. This is one such minilesson. Typically, these turning-point minilessons may merit reinforcement. One way to do this is to closely align your conferences to these critical minilessons. See the conference cited at right from the *Conferring with Primary Writers* book.

Today's minilesson introduced the idea that writing can contain Many Moments rather than a single Small Moment. You may want to carry some examples of this structure with you as you confer. *When I Was Young in the Mountains* is such a story, as is *Alexander and the Terrible, Horrible, No Good, Very Bad Day*; and of course there's *Do Like Kyla*. You'll probably want to find a few children who are just starting new pieces and help them imagine those pieces as Many Moment stories.

Although you probably won't discuss this with your children, these stories will work best if they are united not only by a refrain and a common subject, but also by a shared message or theme. *Do Like Kyla* tells the story of a little sister emulating her big sister from morning till night, with the title as a refrain.

These conferences in *The Conferring Handbook* may be especially helpful today:

▶ *"You Can Use Ellipses to Show Waiting"*
▶ *"Use a Refrain"*
▶ *"I See You're Adding an Exclamation Mark to Your Story Like Mem Fox Does"*

Also, if you have *Conferring with Primary Writers*, you may want to refer to the following conference:

▶ *"Can We Study What This Author Did and Let Her Teach Us Some Lessons?"*

Share several examples of the students' writing and ask students to study them in relation to the chart.

"Let's look at our chart here. We learned that writers need to make choices. Some of us wrote Small Moment stories and others wrote Many Moments pieces.

Where?	What do you see?	Why is she doing this?	We call it . . .	Other Books?
Joshua's Night Whispers	3 dots, 3 times	Slows reader down, something more is going to happen	Dot, dot, dot.	*The Leaving Morning* *Our Stories*
Joshua's Night Whispers	One phrase, 5 times	They keep coming back and they hold the main idea of the story	Comeback lines	*The Leaving Morning* *Our Stories*
The Leaving Morning	Books start with time of day	Instead of starting with weather, starts with time	Time of day	*Joshua's Night Whispers*
The Leaving Morning	Lots of facts, details	Helps us picture what happened	Researches for details	*Make Way for Ducklings*
Joshua's Night Whispers	She lists	So that there is a rhythm to the text	List of things	
Do Like Kyla	Tells lots of moments	To show that all day long the younger sister copies Kyla	Many Moments story	*Joshua by the Sea*

"Listen to these pieces. Let's think about which technique they use." [*Figs. IX-1 and IX-2*]

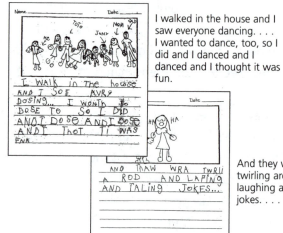

I walked in the house and I saw everyone dancing. . . . I wanted to dance, too, so I did and I danced and I danced and I thought it was fun.

I WALK in The house AND I SOE AVRY DOSING... I WONTH to DOSE TO SO I DID ANDI DOSE ANDI DOSE ANDI THOT TI WAS FNK

And they were twirling around and laughing and telling jokes. . . .

AND THAW WRA TWRLI A ROD AND LAFING AND TALING JOKES...

Fig. IX-1 Casey

Remind children that they can choose a technique from the chart or from any reading to use in their own writing.

"Now look at your own writing from today. What technique did you try? What could you try tomorrow?"

I had a cookie. "Mmmmm," I said.

Now my sister wants some. "Can I have some?" "No!" I said.

My sister got so mad!!!

My sister said please. I said, "Nonononono. . . ." I said.

Fig. IX-2 Alyssa

TRYING A NEW TEXT STRUCTURE: WRITING A MANY MOMENTS STORY

GETTING READY

- *Do Like Kyla*
- A wipe board and dry erase pen (or chart paper and marker)
- Blank charts with squares, see page 86
- *Joshua by the Sea*
- Overhead projector, transparencies of *Joshua by the Sea*
- Copied pages of *Joshua by the Sea*
- See CD-ROM for resources

WHEN CHILDREN BEGIN TO WRITE BOOKS *that contain many moments, the risk is their texts will become a hodgepodge of anything they can think of to say. They may well end up writing books describing a huge watermelon topic—like a trip, their school, or their families—and these texts can be chaotic compilations. This isn't a tragedy—we need to write badly to write well. Children need to tackle the challenge of organizing texts that are not small, chronological narratives, and if, for a while, the resulting texts are less than perfectly arranged, that's okay. But you will want to teach children the importance of selecting bits that go together. In Do Like Kyla, every vignette is another example of how the little sister mimics her big sister, Kyla. The narrator doesn't tell about her school or her sleepover or anything that doesn't go with her main idea.*

This text is also held together by the refrain "I do like Kyla." Since the vignettes all illustrate and contain the repeating refrain, it is a very concrete way to introduce young children to the idea that all the parts of this text relate to the same theme. What an important lesson for young writers to learn! A day at the zoo will be a stronger piece if there is a single theme—"My legs were getting more and more tired as I traveled to the different animals"—bringing unity in the piece.

In this session, with a discussion and a graphic organizer, you'll show children how different small moments are all connected in books like Do Like Kyla and Joshua of the Sea. You'll suggest children choose a unifying thread or a comeback line for their own Many Moments writing.

THE MINILESSON

Connection

Tell students that a thread or an idea runs through Many Moments stories. This thread holds the moments together.

"Yesterday we looked at Angela's Many Moments book, *Do Like Kyla*, and you noticed things about it. I took some notes. You guys said it felt like a list, and that every page was sort of the same. I thought about what you said a lot last night and want us all to think today about how Angela managed to write a Many Moments piece where all the pages are similar—they feel sort of the same—because I think that's the real trick in this kind of writing."

Teaching

Ask students to listen to the start of the book and notice what is different on each page. Fill in a chart that summarizes the different moments.

"Let's look at *Do Like Kyla* again and notice what's the same on each page, and what's different. Let's start by noticing what's different on each page." On the white board, I had already written three blank boxes. I read the first page and filled in the first box with "tapping at the window." Then I read and filled in the next two boxes. Then I drew the top box.

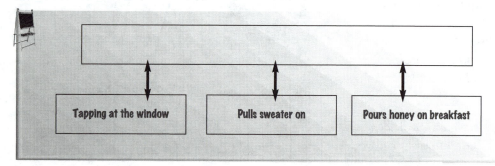

Tapping at the window | Pulls sweater on | Pours honey on breakfast

Teaching often consists of finding significance in what students do. In this instance, the children say something fairly obvious. The pages in Do Like Kyla *are "the same." I get behind this and suggest that writers work hard to make the pages feel sort of the same.*

This minilesson, and specifically this chart, made a big difference in our teaching.

The text begins like this:

> In the morning my big sister Kyla stands at the window tapping at the birds.
> I do like Kyla, only standing on the bed. Kyla pulls her sweater over her head and stretches. I do like Kyla.

Ask children to listen for what is the same in all three moments. Reread this section of the book.

"Now I want to reread these first three moments and let's see *what is the same* in each of these moments. That will give us an idea of the thread that runs throughout the book." I reread the first few pages of the book, changing my voice to emphasize each new moment.

Stop and ask for what is the same in each moment.

"So what is the same in these three moments?" I asked. "Why are all these many moments in one story?"

"On every page she copies Kyla."

"She likes to do the same thing as her sister."

"Each moment she is copying her."

"The comeback line is the same thing on every page."

"What you are saying is so smart. Angela Johnson wrote a lot of moments, but they weren't about all different things. The moments were held together by one idea, one thread, one comeback line." I filled in the top of the diagram with the overarching theme. "'Angela only tells what she does to be like her sister Kyla.'"

I try to find a concrete, simple way to show children that Angela Johnson has written her many moments in a patterned way, giving unity to her book.

Notice the way this minilesson takes your last few minilessons a step further.

Active Engagement

Now have students try to notice similar features in another text.

"I want to read you another Many Moments Angela Johnson book, and I'm going to ask you and your partner to think how you'd fill in the same chart for this book. So here is a blank chart." I flipped the paper on the chart tablet

In the morning my big sister Kyla stands at the window, tapping at the birds.
I do like Kyla, only standing on the bed.

to reveal another blank chart. "Now listen to this book. First just listen, then I'll reread it again." I read *Joshua by the Sea*, showing it on the overhead as I read.

> I am Joshua,
> in the sun, sand,
> and by the sea.
> I am Joshua with Mama
> and Daddy beside me.
> under the umbrella,
> seagulls, and blue sky.
> Beside my sister
> on the rocks up high.
> I am Joshua running free.
> I am Joshua by the sea.

"I'll reread just the first page. You'll need to use the pictures as well as the words to help you figure out how you could fill in this box for page one." I gave them time to talk, then used their input to fill in the box. I continued reading, then again gave them time to talk, and again filled in the chart with their input until it looked like this.

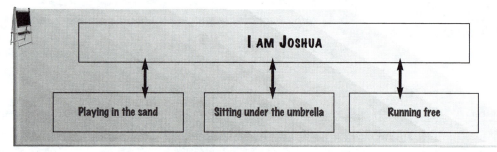

Link

Send students off, reminding them that if they write a Many Moments story, they'll want to have an important idea in their story that can become their thread.

"Today, if you are starting a new story, you may decide to try writing a many moments piece. If you do, remember that your big idea should come through to your reader. If you write a Many Moments story, you will want to choose a comeback line that reminds the readers of the big idea of your story. Pick something important."

I read this book aloud twice because it's a new book for the children and I think it's difficult for anyone to think about the craftsmanship in a book while reading the text for the first time.

You can demonstrate that this chart is one that children can use again and again by showing that it is applicable to many texts. Meanwhile you are visibly illustrating the concept of thematic unity, although of course you don't use the term!

For today, as for yesterday, there is no question but that you'll need to confer in support of today's minilesson. Your goal is for some children to choose a narrative (the subway trip, the visit to the zoo, the birthday party) that contains a series of events. Early on during today's workshop, you may want to ask, "Who thinks they'll write a Many Moments piece?" so you can get to those children. The others should be fine without a lot of help from you. If one child tells about all the animals he saw at the zoo, you can help him realize that his book would benefit from a shared message about those animals. Perhaps on each page, he pretends he could adopt that animal as his own, or on each page, he notices a beautiful feature about the animal, or looks for evidence of a baby.

These conferences in *The Conferring Handbook* may be especially helpful today:

▶ *"You Can Use Ellipses to Show Waiting"*

▶ *"Use a Refrain"*

▶ *"I See You're Adding an Exclamation Mark to Your Story Like Mem Fox Does"*

Also, if you have *Conferring with Primary Writers,* you may want to refer to the conferences in part five.

Share the writing of two students and let the class help you fill out the same charts for each.

"Writers, listen to the pieces some of your classmates have been writing. As I read the next piece, let's try to fill in our chart. Let's listen for what is the same on each page and for what's different on each page." I read and filled in the chart.

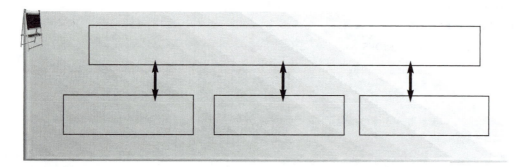

Then I read another of the children's stories and together, the children and I filled in the same-shaped chart.

▸ You could have the class think back to an important event about which your class could write a Many Moments story. Any trip would work, as long as the class decided what the one thing would be that they wanted to show. This could be as simple as "we had fun." Use the chart to plan all the pages of the text.

▸ You could read students a piece of your writing and ask them to help you bring out something that could be the same across all your pages.

▸ You could show the class other Many Moments stories. One obvious one is *When I Was Young in the Mountains* by Cynthia Rylant (which isn't actually a story, but a list). It contains many moments held together by a refrain.

TRYING A NEW TEXT STRUCTURE: WRITING A MANY MOMENTS STORY WITH DETAILS

GETTING READY

▶ Copies of a piece of student writing for everyone to hold and study as an example

▶ Hard surface to write on (folder, wipe boards, clipboard)

▶ Pens for students

● See CD-ROM for resources

GROWTH ALWAYS INVOLVES TWO STEPS FORWARD, ONE STEP BACK. *When children are invited to write pieces that no longer have a very tight chronological focus, it is inevitable that they'll revert to writing in generalities. You can predict, therefore, that you'll need to highlight the continuing importance of detail. Do Like Kyla is a perfect text for teaching children that writers can make Many Moments pieces that continue to be very detailed.*

Today you'll show how one child in the class has included details in his Many Moments story so that everyone can add his examples to Angela's.

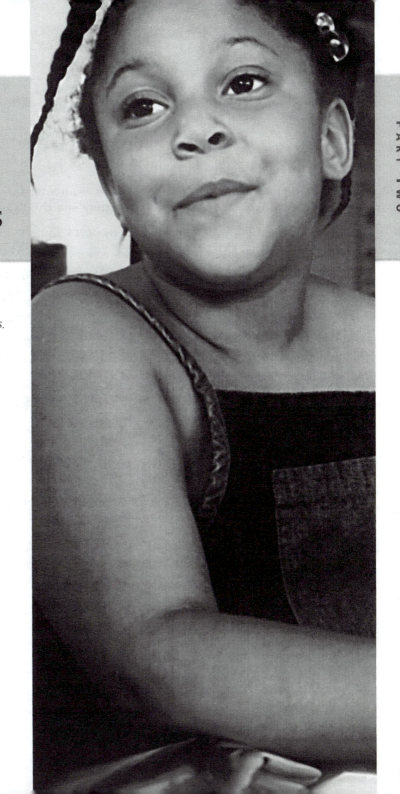

The Minilesson

Connection

Tell the students that when they write Many Moments stories, they risk forgetting to write with detail. Tell them today they'll study one child's effort to write with detail.

"Yesterday I worked with a group of students and we were thinking about how we could keep the power of small moments when we write Many Moments stories. We didn't want to lose the details that show our readers what we have been experiencing, feeling, and thinking. Some of your classmates have been working to keep details in their Many Moments pieces. I thought we could study Patrick's writing to learn tips for keeping details in our pieces."

Teaching

Show children how you notice the way one child wove details into each section of a Many Moments piece.

"As I read each part of Patrick's piece, I am going to notice how Patrick says *a lot about each moment*. He writes about a visit to the zoo. He tells about one moment at the reptile house and one moment with the elephants. Listen for how much he says about the first one, the snake moment."

> On a lovely sunny day my family went to the zoo.
> First we went to the reptile house. We saw lots of different
> snakes. They looked like they were sleeping. We saw vine snakes and
> sidewinder snakes. I wanted to go to the bird house. I asked my mom.
> She said, "Be patient!"

"I'm noticing that Patrick didn't just say, 'First we went to the snakes. They were nice.' He told us *details*, didn't he? Listen again and see if you can notice details." I reread the page from Patrick's book. "He told us that the snakes were sleeping and he listed specific kinds of snakes. Then he didn't just say, 'I wanted to move on.' He said even that with details: 'I wanted to go to the bird house. I asked my mom.'"

It is predictable that when children write Many Moments pieces, they'll revert to the unfocused, underdeveloped stories we've tried to avoid. The last thing you want is to lose all the lovely detail that has made such a difference in your children's writing. It's clear, then, that after introducing the concept of Many Moments pieces, you'll need to teach children that each moment needs to be developed by use of detail.

Over and over, I highlight a strategy by saying what the writing could have been like without it.

Active Engagement

Give students a piece of writing. Ask them to underline parts that show details.

"I'm going to read the next page of Patrick's writing and give you a copy of that page too. Would you listen while I read this next page and on your copy, underline details you see Patrick using?" Then I read this [*Fig. XI-1*].

> When we walked in the bird house the first thing we saw was the horned owl it had razor sharp claws and a killer beak and do not forget the mighty wings. . . . I felt like I wanted to dive into the cage but I couldn't. It is illegal.

Convene the students and collect their observations.

"Show your partner the details you notice Patrick using."

"He said the horned owl had razor sharp claws and a killer beak."

"And he said how he felt like he wanted to dive in the cage!"

"He said about all the types of birds in the other house."

"Guys, may I stop you? Do you see that Patrick didn't just write, 'I went to the zoo. I saw snakes. Then I went to the bird house. I saw birds.'? He *showed* what he saw at the snake house and then *showed* what he saw at the bird house. He wrote with details."

Link

Remind students that when they write Many Moments pieces, it's still important to write with details.

"As you all go off to write today, you have another mentor, Patrick, to help you remember that even if you are writing a Many Moments piece, the details we've always cared about still count. Try putting details in your own writing, just as Patrick and Angela do."

This piece of writing is a good one for a lot of reasons that are worth naming. Another time you could return to this piece to teach other qualities of good writing. Notice the writer's energy and enthusiasm. These matter.

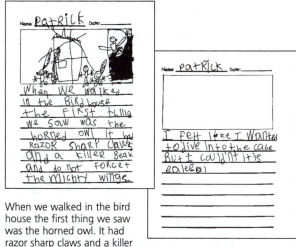

When we walked in the bird house the first thing we saw was the horned owl. It had razor sharp claws and a killer beak and do not forget the mighty wings. . . .
I felt like I wanted to dive into the cage but I couldn't. It is illegal.

Fig. XI-1   Patrick

TIME TO CONFER

Sometimes it's helpful to carry a short stack of mentor texts with you as you confer and to use those texts as you co-teach. Ask children, "What are you working on as a writer?" or "What are you trying to do?" and then follow this up with, "Can you show me where you've tried that?" Then say, "Sometimes when I'm trying to do a particular thing, I look for an author who has done what I want to do." That comment ensures that you are teaching children a strategy they can use often, on other days. Then say, "I think Angela did what you are trying to do. Let me show you where." "Soon you and the child will be looking at the mentor text together, and you'll say to the student, "What do you notice about what she's done? Could you try that?" See the conferences cited at right.

This conference in *The Conferring Handbook* may be especially helpful today:

▶ *"I See You're Adding an Exclamation Mark to Your Story Like Mem Fox Does"*

Also, if you have *Conferring with Primary Writers*, you may want to refer to the following conferences:

▶ "Let's Look at Your Lead and Your Ending"
▶ "As a Reader, I'd Love to Hear More About This"

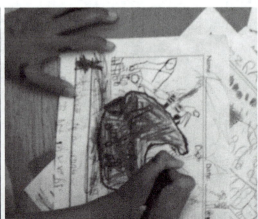

AFTER-THE-WORKSHOP SHARE

Ask children to choose a part of their writing that they love to share.

"Do you remember how, at the start of the year, you guys brought small treasures to school—acorns and pretty stones—and showed them during 'Show and Tell'? Today we're going to have another show and tell. We're going to bring out our small treasures and show them to each other. But they'll be small treasures we find in our own writing. Before we start our sharing, could you reread your writing and find a detail you love, a detail that is a small treasure, and would you star it?"

The room was silent while children reread. Then, for a while, a few children shared their small treasures with the class.

When children do this, remember that your job is to help all the class listen in such a way that the readers' words leave an imprint. Model intent, responsive listening, and expect it. Use phrases like, "Eyes on . . . " or, to the reader, "Wait till you can hear a pin drop. Read it like this is gold."

To devote more days to the importance of writing with detail, you could try the following ideas.

▸ Reread a part in *Do Like Kyla* to have students to think about the details Angela Johnson includes in the moment. For example, Kyla kisses the sunbeam as it lands on her dog's head, and she wears purple snow boots to crunch, crunch the snow.

▸ Go back to a piece of shared writing and think about which details you could add to the page. You'll have lots of pieces from earlier in the year that could benefit from more detail.

▸ Talk to students about the fact that as writers grow, we need paper that provides more lines for our words. Suggest they look back over the year and notice the way their paper has—or hasn't—changed.

STUDYING NEW AUTHORS AS MENTORS

GETTING READY

- Sticky notes ready for noticing craft
- Selected texts, enough for two books per child
- *Shortcut* by Donald Crews
- See CD-ROM for resources

THIS SESSION MARKS THE START *of a new part in this unit. After studying one author's writing process and craft, children need to realize that the point of all this is not Angela Johnson. The point is that all of us, as writers, can have private tutors at our disposal. All we need to do is to locate a text or an author we admire, then study what the author has done, speculate on why, and then emulate the technique. For the final week of this author study, we will invite children to find their own mentor authors.*

You may want to steer children toward some books that you believe will be especially helpful mentor texts. Look for texts written in such a way that children will notice and want to emulate the techniques the authors have used. You may want texts with fairly obvious features (sound effects, print in the illustrations, a pattern to the language, and so on). Ideally, each child has two somewhat similar books by one author so the child is engaged in an author study not a text study. You could plan this so there is a pair of kids studying one author and another pair studying another author. Later you could merge two sets of partnerships for more talk and more energy. These authors (among others) should work well: Byrd Baylor, Eric Carle, Joy Cowley, Donald Crews, Lois Ehlert, Judith Viorst, and Charlotte Zolotow.

In this session, you will ask children to turn to a new author and begin to notice and think about characteristics of that author's book in that same way that they have looked at Angela Johnson's books.

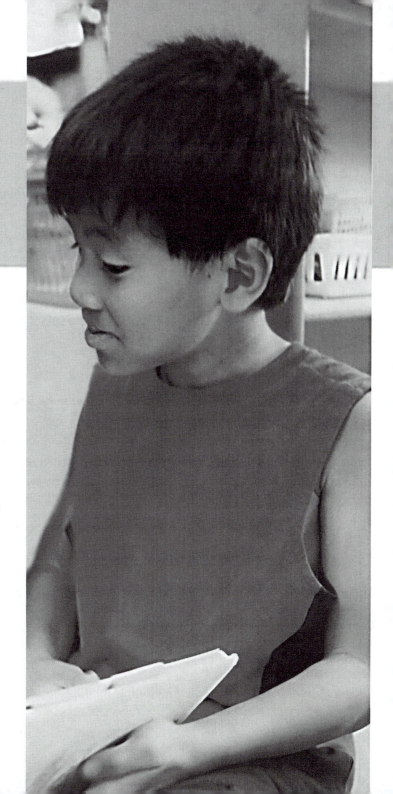

THE MINILESSON

Connection

Tell writers that in the same way they have learned from Angela Johnson, they can learn from any author they choose.

"Writers, we have learned so much from studying Angela Johnson's books. Today I want to be sure you know that, as writers, you and I can study *any* author. Any day, when you want a tip about how to write well, all you have to do is reach out to a book you love and then read that book like a writer, thinking, 'What works here?' or 'How did he (or she) make this?' or 'What did the author do that I could try?'"

Teaching

Demonstrate that this is true by taking another book and starting the same process you went through as a class with Angela's books.

"Let's just take another book. Let's take Donald Crews' *Shortcut*. I will reread it aloud and I want you to watch how I read this book, thinking about what Donald Crews does as a writer. Later today and tomorrow, you'll be doing this on your own with new books."

"Notice I have my sticky notes. When I notice something I like, I am going to put a sticky note on it and think, 'What is he doing here? Why does he do this?'"

Open the book, begin to read, and mark something the author does that seems interesting. Begin to muse aloud about why the author may have chosen to write this way.

"Wow, right here he fills the first page with the sound words 'KLACK KLACK KLACK.'" Amanda inserted a sticky note. In an aside whisper she said, "Now I'm going to try to figure out *why* he starts his book with sound effects. Hmmm. . . . I wonder why Crews puts these big huge sound words here? Maybe he wants us to hear that noise as we read and to wonder what was making that big noise."

I act as if children definitely want suggestions on how to write well. The questions I suggest here are important ones.

This is a spectacular text to teach children to pay attention to an author's techniques. The book is short, it is a personal narrative, and Crews uses very easily identifiable techniques, particularly the use of large sound words embedded in the pictures. The book offers a fabulous example of dramatic tension.

Continue noticing enticing features of the book and musing about the author's intentions.

Amanda turned the page and read the next page out loud. "You know what I see right away? 'Dot, dot, dot'! Just like Angela Johnson!" She added a second sticky note. "Let me think. . . . Why does Donald Crews use these? Hmmm. . . . I think he is trying to slow down his beginning. To get us to pay careful attention."

Active Engagement

Ask children to try, with their partners, to go through the same process you just went through.

"So I'm going to stop now. I'm going to give one person from each partnership a book (other books are at your seats). There are sticky notes inside the book I'm giving you. Would you and your partner make observations about your book? Do this on your own, right here on the rug."

After a pause long enough for children to find some things in their books, ask a few to talk with you about what they've found so far.

Amanda approached two partners who were studying Crews' *Sail Away.* "Guys, what are you finding?"

Johan: "We noticed that he has sounds words."

Peter: "Yeah 'putt, putt, putt.'"

Johan: "He also has 'dot, dot, dot' just like Angela Johnson."

Peter: "Yeah and he makes big words!"

"He does? That's interesting. You two have told me what he does. Are you also remembering to ask yourselves *why* he might do these things?" They looked sheepish. "Would you guys go back and for each thing you notice, be sure to ask, 'Why?'"

Peter turned the pages back, and they took turns reading the pages. "Why does Donald Crews use 'dot, dot, dot' here?"

Johan: "Because he wants to make it slow."

They turned the page and noticed "WHOOSH!"

"Here the boat goes 'Whoosh!'" Peter noted. "Not 'putt, putt, putt. . . .'"

Johan said, "Now the sounds change to show it is going fast. It is changing."

It is important to echo the process you demonstrated with Angela Johnson. Amanda is following the same sequence and using the same words to study Crews' book as we used to study Angela Johnson's book.

Amanda doesn't read Crews' entire book aloud. Instead, she uses a few pages from that book as a demonstration and now sets kids up to try similar work.

Sail Away is a great book to study in this way. Crews uses very few words and a lot of techniques that children will spot easily.

The most important thing is to ask, "Why?"

Link

Sum up for the class, and remind kids that what they've learned can serve their own writing.

"We have noticed more things! Some kids noticed other authors using 'dot, dot, dot.'" Some kids saw that you can also make a list by using commas! We noticed different beginnings that sounded interesting. As you go off to write today, please continue to study the books I've put on your writing spaces. Learn from these books like you learned from Angela Johnson's books. And then let this new writer give you ideas for your own writing!"

You needn't summarize or elicit observations. Children benefit more from the work they did than from your summaries of that work.

TIME TO CONFER

You'll want to prepare for your conferences today by rereading your conferring checklist and having it with you. Today's minilesson essentially says to children, "Go for it!" and invites them to work with independence on the very concepts you've tried to teach. You'll want to be ready to notice what they do, and almost do, on their own, and to teach to support what you see.

You'll also want to have some books on hand in which the authors have used some easily replicable techniques. The following titles are examples.

Book	Easy-to-Copy Technique
Paul Showers, *The Listening Walk*	Sound effects
Eric Carle, *Very Hungry Caterpillar*	Speech balloons, flaps and cutouts
Lois Ehlert, *Feathers for Lunch*	Speech balloons, sound effects
Eric Hill, *Where's Spot?*	Question/Answer Flaps

 These conferences in *The Conferring Handbook* may be especially helpful today:

▶ *"You Can Use Ellipses to Show Waiting"*
▶ *"Use a Refrain"*
▶ *"I See You're Adding an Exclamation Mark to Your Story Like Mem Fox Does"*

Also, if you have *Conferring with Primary Writers*, you may want to refer to the conferences in part five.

After-the-Workshop Share

Ask a child to share the work he has done under the mentorship of a new author.

"Brandon read *The Relatives Came* by Cynthia Rylant. I want you to listen to Brandon's Many Moments book. Brandon, will you share with us what you did in your writing?"

"My story is about going to Central Park. I love it there. It is my favorite park. I tried to make my ending like Cynthia Rylant."

"How did you do that?"

"I wrote about a Many Moments piece. Then when it was over, I was dreaming about it in my home."

"Is that what Rylant does?"

Brandon responded by reading Rylant's ending!

> And when they were finally home in Virginia,
> they crawled into their silent, soft beds and dreamed about
> the next summer.

"Now read us your piece. Let's listen to Brandon's ending and let's see what we notice." Brandon read it aloud. [*Fig. XII-1*]

Ask the class to notice ways in which the child's writing was similar to the published writing.

Mariko: "I like your repeating line. Central Park is important to your story."

Sasha: "It is the same as *The Relatives Came* because she was dreaming and so were you."

"Writers, turn to your partner and share what *you* did today in your writing. Show each other both your piece of writing and also the books you studied. Find what is the same."

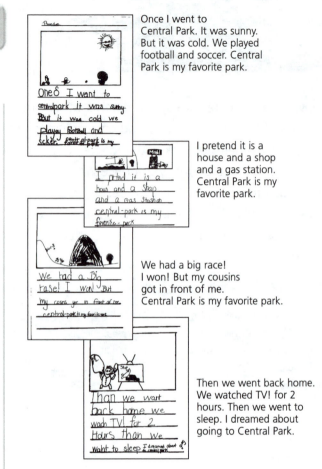

Once I went to Central Park. It was sunny. But it was cold. We played football and soccer. Central Park is my favorite park.

I pretend it is a house and a shop and a gas station. Central Park is my favorite park.

We had a big race! I won! But my cousins got in front of me. Central Park is my favorite park.

Then we went back home. We watched TV! for 2 hours. Then we went to sleep. I dreamed about going to Central Park.

Fig. XII-1   Brandon

We set children up, letting them know the angle we hope they take as they listen.

If Children Need More Time

This minilesson will have been fairly self-explanatory, but the work it launches could definitely require more time (and should not need a whole lot of instructional guidance). You can do some fairly lightweight minilessons for the next day or two that devote more time to this. The most obvious way to extend this minilesson is to have tomorrow's minilesson involve a reiteration of today's and an emphasis on children reading and talking more about why the author has used a technique (most will notice techniques, sticky-note them, and move on). You could make your point by continuing to read *Sail Away*. If you are going to do this, be sure children bring their books with them to the minilesson (perhaps securing them in their writing folders).

EMULATING AUTHORS IN WAYS THAT MATTER

GETTING READY

- Book the children are studying with an obvious feature marked, such as Eric Hill's *Where's Spot?* with its flaps marked
- Donald Crews' *Shortcut*
- Your own piece of writing, with an idea for four to six sound effects that could be added
- Stack of four to six sticky notes, each holding a sound effect that could be inserted into your story
- See CD-ROM for resources

OFTEN ONE MINILESSON IS A CORRECTION OF ANOTHER. *We teach children ellipses . . . and we then have to teach them how to keep ellipses from swamping their pieces. This minilesson is a correction on the one before it. When you first invite children to notice the craft in books, they tend to notice the zany, obvious features. They'll notice the holes and flaps in Eric Carle's writing, the sound effects in Lois Ehlert's writing, the large print and ellipses in Donald Crews' writing, the chapters in Cynthia Rylant's Henry and Mudge series, and so forth. The problem is they can add holes, flaps, sound effects, and chapters without improving their writing. Now you'll nudge them to look beneath the obvious features and to try to name what the features accomplish.*

In this session, you'll demonstrate for kids what a haphazard addition of a new kind of writing can look like, and then you'll ask them to join you in adding a meaningful, revised addition to your writing.

THE MINILESSON

Connection

Remind kids of how exciting studying authors has been so far and how proud they can be of themselves.

"I can't wait for writing time today because so many of you are making tons of discoveries about your author. I can't believe you guys are actually doing author studies on your own! Congratulations. I was thinking this would be good work for *fifth* graders and that you wouldn't be able to do it. But my gosh! I think *all* of you noticed something in your authors' books. Did you? Thumbs up if you, on your own, noticed a technique *your* author used. Wow!"

Tell kids they need to do more than notice and imitate interesting features of the writing they are studying.

Are you ready for more fifth-grade work? You are? Okay. Here's what I want to say. Sometimes when we study authors, we notice the most obvious things (like in this *Where's Spot?* book, we notice flaps) and then we put flaps into our writing and it is really cool because now our book has flaps just like *Where's Spot?* has flaps. My book could say 'I sled down the (and under the flap—the word *hill*).' But you know what? I'm not sure that flap would have made it a better story at all!"

Tell kids they need to think about why the interesting feature is there and what it accomplishes.

"Sometimes we notice things an author has done and we do those things and our writing gets no better at all! So today and tomorrow I want to teach you a few ways to make sure that what we learn really helps our writing. Today, we need to spend more time thinking about *why* an author has used flaps (or sound effects or big print or whatever it is). We need to ask, 'What is the main, big thing he or she is trying to get across to readers?' and we need to see that the author uses a bunch of techniques—like a bunch of tools—to do that main job."

It's smart to build up your children's identities. Sometimes, naming what children have done or have almost done is the most powerful teaching we can do.

It would be easy to forgive the fact that reading-writing connections for kindergarteners and first graders result in flaps that don't really improve the quality of a text at all—but I believe in being direct and ambitious. There's not much risk in going for the gold!

Teaching

Demonstrate for kids an unhelpful use of the technique they've found in a previous session.

"Let's look again at Crews' *Shortcut*. Remember the first pages?" I read them.

> We looked . . .
> We listened . . .
> We decided to take
> the shortcut home.
>
> We should have taken the road.
> But it was late, and it was
> getting dark, so we
> started down the track.

| Whoo |

> We knew when the passenger trains
> passed. But the freight trains
> didn't run on schedule.
> They might come at any time.
> We should have taken the road.

"You could read this book and just say, 'He uses sound effects' and then you could plop them into *your* story any ol' place. Let's say your story at first looked like this,"

> I was sledding down the hill.
> I saw a kid and a dad. I couldn't steer.
> I hit them. The dad got mad.

"Soon it could look like this," I said as I added the sticky notes holding sound effects.

| Brr! | | Wow |

> I was sledding down the hill.

> I saw a kid and a dad. I couldn't steer. | Yikes! |

| Help |

> I hit them. The dad got mad.

What a beautiful text this is! Read it well, and read it often.

The book continues to show the oncoming train, with the sound effects growing in size and impact as the train approaches. Read a bit beyond the excerpt I quote here.

When I'm trying to teach something fairly complicated to very young children, I make sure my examples aren't subtle in the least. Most little kids will comprehend that my use of sound effects leaves something to be desired.

Demonstrate for kids the way you think about why the author writes as he or she does.

"But it would be smarter to look really closely at Crews' story and think, '*Why* does he use sound effects? What is the main thing he really wants to get across to the reader?'"

"So I'm going to reread his text again and think about that." I did. "Hmmm. It seems to me he wants the reader to feel what he felt when he heard the train coming. He wants our hearts to beat, he wants us to go, 'Oh no! Oh no!' And he wants us to get more worried as time goes by. That's why his sound effects start small and then get larger, then larger. . . . He's building up the excitement."

Demonstrate the way you ask, "What am I trying to show my reader?" and use a technique for a purpose.

"Now I have to look at my story and think, 'What do I really want to get across to my reader?' What I really want my readers to know is how awful I felt when I ran into the people. So I'm not going to add 'Brrr' or 'Wow!'" I pulled those and other sticky notes off. "I can't just add any ol' sound effects. I'm going to add what the dad yelled. I'm going to add, 'He screamed, 'YOU FOOL!'" and I made that big so you hear his voice too."

> I was sledding down the hill.
> I saw a kid and a dad. I couldn't steer.
> I hit them. The dad got mad.
> He screamed, "YOU FOOL!"

Active Engagement

Ask the class to help you revise your text, again using the technique to convey your meaning.

"I might add one more sound effect, but I want to be sure I do so in ways that show how I felt when I hit the kid. I put the dad yelling, but I don't yet have me feeling sad. Hmm. . . . Can you talk to your partner and see if you can find a way for me to use Crews' technique of sound effects to show how sad I felt?"

After a few minutes of talk, I called on a few children.

"You could add crying noises and say 'sorry.'"

"So how would it go?"

This is a true story. Usually when I am writing a text for children, I go for the truth because somehow kids can tell.

"Sniff, sniff. Soo . . . Sorry . . . Sniff. Sniff."

"Or you could say, 'I'm sorry,' but make the letters tiny tiny tiny to show how you felt."

"These are both great ideas. Thanks."

Link

Sum up for the children what they need to do in their own writing to apply what they have learned from other authors and to make their writing better.

"Time for you guys to get going. This is not easy work, writers. But what I am going to ask you to do today is to revise whatever revisions you made yesterday. You'll do these steps:

"Go back and study where your author used a technique you've used. Look really closely and think, 'Why did the author do it this way?' Try to get smart ideas in your head."

"Then, look again at your work. Think, 'I could do this even better.' Use a new sticky note on top of the old one and write a new try on top of the old try. Make sure your revisions make your writing better."

These are great ideas. The only reason I was able to elicit these wonderful examples is that I listened in while children talked to their partners and heard a few children making especially powerful suggestions. I also interacted with them, eliciting a bit more detail so that by the time I called on these children within the minilesson, they were more than ready!

These are complex and multi-faceted directions. I know as I say them that some children will be able to do this, and others will need a lot of support.

TIME TO CONFER

This unit of study is nearing an end, so it's a good time for you to let children be extra inventive and extra independent. If two children come to you proposing that they write a series book like the books they're reading during reading time, why not? They may have to do much of it at home, but what better play date can you imagine? And if a child follows a favorite author into fiction into retelling a fairy tale, emphasize the shared aspects of what they're doing (learning from their own author studies) and give them some free rein. Very soon, you'll ask them to prepare for an author celebration.

Meanwhile today's minilesson requires support. Help children to reconsider their reading-writing connections. Above all, you want them to think, "What am I trying to make readers feel or think?" and, "How can I use this technique (flaps, sound effects, repetitions, etc.) to be sure the piece does what I want it to do?"

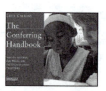

These conferences in *The Conferring Handbook* may be especially helpful today:

▶ *"You Can Use Ellipses to Show Waiting"*
▶ *"Use a Refrain"*
▶ *"I See You're Adding an Exclamation Mark to Your Story Like Mem Fox Does"*

Also, if you have *Conferring with Primary Writers*, you may want to refer to the conferences in part five.

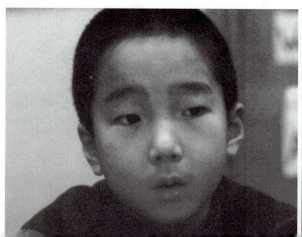

AFTER-THE-WORKSHOP SHARE

Ask children to have a partner read their writing. Ask the writer to check to make sure the reader is getting the intended message, revising when necessary.

"Writers, you've all used so many techniques to help readers really feel what you want them to feel. I think it'd be important for you to check out if your stories are doing the job you want them to do."

"So I'm going to put you together in twos with kids who haven't heard your stories recently. I want the reader (not the writer) to read aloud a story. Writers, you listen and see if the reader has any trouble reading your story. If so, you probably have to fix some spelling or some punctuation. And see if the reader has the right tone in his or her voice. If not, see if you can change the words on the paper so readers read them well. Okay? Off you go."

It's nearing the end of the unit so this is an especially good time to spotlight the importance of writing for readers. Using punctuation is one part of writing for readers.

- You will definitely have stories to share of children who adopt a mentor author and try to write like that author. Tell one of these stories in a way that highlights whatever you want to highlight. For example, you may want to teach children to look very closely at what their author did. At first, a child might think that Eric Hill simply used flaps on every page, but a closer look suggests every page contains a question, and the flaps are there for a purpose—to hide the answer.

- Life is full of stories about people who emulate heroes. Tell a story about an athlete, singer, painter, or teacher who studies the work of a mentor and then tries to incorporate that person's techniques into his or her own work.

- Be sure that when you talk about mentor authors who can be emulated, you cite a child's work as well as published author's work.

TURNING TO AUTHORS FOR SPECIFIC HELP

GETTING READY

▶ Your own writing on an overhead or chart paper, ripe for the revision you have planned

▶ Set of familiar books the children have all been studying

▶ See CD-ROM for resources

IN THE LAST SESSION, YOU ASKED STUDENTS TO THINK HARD *about authors' reasons for putting features into their texts. Students focused on the effects the authors created through these special features. In this session, you will tell writers that another way to improve their writing is to think first about what their own work needs and, only then, to find a writer who could help them do whatever their work needs.*

You'll demonstrate in this session the importance of rereading your own writing to think of what might make it better. Then you'll show how you turn to other writers for ideas on how to improve your writing. You'll ask children to do the same for their own writing.

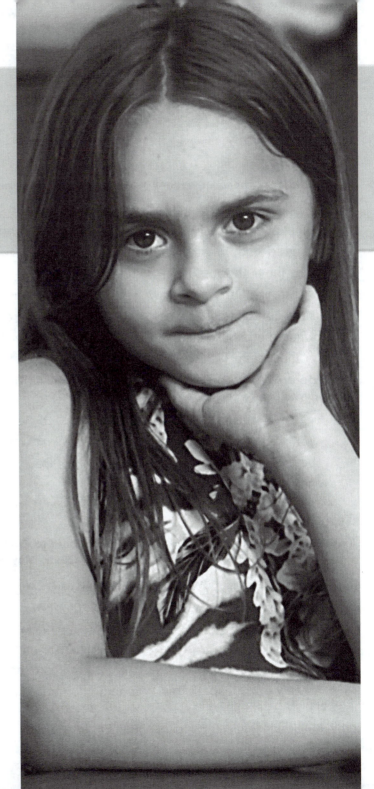

Connection

Tell the children there are several ways to let an author help you with your writing.

"Yesterday we talked about how we can be sure we use the techniques other authors teach us in ways that improve our writing. I taught you that we need to study what the author was mainly trying to do, and notice how and why the author used a technique. Remember when I just added any ol' sound effects like 'Brrr' and 'Wow!' my sledding story didn't really improve? But my story got a lot better when you and I used sound effects to show what I felt when the father yelled at me. So one hint is to really study how and why an author uses a technique."

Teach children that when writers try to make their writing better, they look for an author who uses a technique that would help.

"A second hint is this. Often it helps to start by thinking about *your* writing (not your authors) and to think, 'What would make my writing even better?' Then and only then do you think, 'Do I know another writer who could help me do this?'"

Teaching

Tell the children that today you'll show them how to look at their own writing to see what it needs, so that when they turn to an author, they are looking for specific help.

"Let me show you what this means. I have these books near me—books I know well. I have Angela Johnson's books, and Donald Crews' *Shortcut*, and I have Virginia Lee Burton's *Mike Mulligan and His Steam Shovel*. But I keep these books over here." I pushed them away. "They are like a row of teachers. I can go to them if I need help just like you can come to me or to Amanda when you need writing help. But first you try to do things on your own, and I do too."

This is high-level work, and some of your children will be able to hear this but not able to translate it into practice. That's okay. Whereas the content we teach in the early minilessons is usually something everyone incorporates into their writing, by this time in a unit, two or three minilessons are often more tailored to our stronger writers. Meanwhile, we use conferring and strategy lessons to teach the writers who need extra help and support.

I love the idea that a row of books is like a row of teachers! Having the books on hand—and physically pushing them to the side—helps children take in what I'm saying.

Read your writing aloud. Demonstrate how you think about what would improve your piece.

"Okay. Here is my writing. I'm going to reread it and think, 'What's the big thing I am saying? How could I say it better?'"

> I went on a trip.
> I packed a lot of things.
> My suitcase was very full.
> It was heavy.

"Hmm. I think I am trying to show that I packed and packed. I packed *a lot* of things. So now I'm going to think about if any of my 'teachers' could help." I gestured to the small shelf of books. "Am I going to look for suitcases (like the suitcases in my story) in these books? No! I'm looking for how these authors, my teachers, show what it's like when *they* keep doing something and doing it."

Demonstrate for the children how to choose which author to study and how to take some advice from the books.

"I wonder if Angela does that in *Joshua's Night Whispers*?" I reread. "Hmm. She could have said, 'Joshua walked a lot of places. He walked a whole lot of places'—like I said, 'I packed a lot of things,' and instead she listed the places. That's one thing. Maybe she is telling me I should list what I packed."

"And wait a minute, wait! In *Mike Mulligan*, when he dug that hole, it doesn't just say 'a lot of people came to watch.' It says, 'Mrs. McGillicuddy, Henry B. Swap, and the Town Constable came over to see what was happening, and they stayed to watch.' Then it says, 'the fire department and the children across the street who couldn't keep their eyes on their lessons and the teacher who called a long recess came.' Wow. Burton is teaching me I should give a very detailed list of what I packed. I could say, 'I packed my sweatshirt with paint stains on it, and the hair brush I got for my birthday' (I better put a comma in like I see in *Mike Mulligan* too. What good help I'm getting from these authors!")

This section of this minilesson is challenging. I want children to realize that authors think not only about what they're writing but also about how they're writing, and usually our reading-writing connections occur around the how, or the craft, of our writing. A published author could create the mood of a brilliant spring day, and if I am writing about a stormy day, I could still benefit from learning how an author creates a mood. A writer could tell about a character running and running and running, faster and faster, and I could use those lessons to help me write about eating and eating and eating, more and more. Kids won't instantly "get" this, but a surprising number catch on.

I find that these excerpts from Mike Mulligan *are really helpful. Notice that I convey my message by showing several different places where authors use a similar craft technique to create the same effect.*

Active Engagement

Retell the steps children need to take to do this work with their own writing.

"The first step is to reread a piece of your writing. And you need to ask, 'What is the main thing I'm trying to show my readers? How could I do this better?' *Then* you go to your author teachers."

Help children practice this using a short piece of writing.

"Let's practice. Let's pretend you were writing about how you skated around the circle quickly. Let's say your piece said this:"

I skated quickly. Then I went home.

"Let's pretend you wanted to help readers feel the speed. Would you and your partner think of an author from our stack who could help you? I'm thinking of a page of *Mike Mulligan.*"

Never had he dug so hard and so well . . ."Hurry, Mike Mulligan! Hurry! Hurry!" shouted the little boy. There's not much more time! Dirt was flying everywhere, and the smoke and steam were so thick. . . .

"Should this writer add dirt and smoke into this skating story?"

"No!"

"You're right. What might he say? Turn to your partner and tell what he could say."

"He skated fast, fast, fast. 'Hurry! Hurry!' He skated so fast he was dizzy."

"Okay, that's one way, and you all could think of others."

Link

Remind students that they need to reread their writing, thinking about what they want to show their reader.

"The important thing is to start by rereading your own writing and thinking, 'What am I trying to show the reader?' Why don't you get started doing that now?"

After you take children through all the steps of a process, you need to figure out how to rewind back to the first step and retell that step. You need to set them up so they can start with just that one step, and then they'll be off and running.

This is only possible because the children know these books backwards and forwards. When Hemingway was asked, "How do you learn to write?" he answered, "Read Anna Karenina, read Anna Karenina, read Anna Karenina."

Here, again, I rewind to the first step and scaffold that step.

Time to Confer

On these, the final days of your unit of study, you'll probably want to do a few things that you'll do at the end of each of your units.

- Help children get ready for the publication party.
- Especially support children who struggle or who've been absent, so that they'll be proud of their work when it is published.
- Help children look back on all their work across this unit and articulate what they've learned that they want to carry with them.
- Assess what children have learned and tailor your plans for the next unit based on your decisions about work that needs to continue and work that can be pronounced "done!" Do this in conjunction with your assessment rubric and your conferring chart.

These conferences in *The Conferring Handbook* may be especially helpful today:

- *"You Can Use Ellipses to Show Waiting"*
- *"Use a Refrain"*
- *"I See You're Adding an Exclamation Mark to Your Story Like Mem Fox Does"*

Also, if you have *Conferring with Primary Writers*, you may want to refer to the conferences in part five.

Ask the children to share their writing intentions with their partners, and direct them to plan ways with each other to make their writing stronger.

"Writers, so many of you have been thinking about the big things you are trying to show your readers. That is smart. We have to think about what we want our readers to feel and understand about our stories. Sophie worked on this today and she wanted her audience to know that she was scared about getting her ears pierced. As a writer it is her job to write her story in a way that makes us feel and understand how she felt. So Sophie went back to add and to change parts in her writing. Could you turn to your writing partner and talk about what you are trying to show your reader in your piece? Point to places where you might add things to make your reader understand what you are trying to show. Partners, you are like writing teachers, listen carefully to your partner and see how you can help them. Give them some smart advice."

EDITING FOR PUBLICATION

GETTING READY

▶ Trouble List of words
▶ Clipboards
▶ Paper, pens
⊙ See CD-ROM for resources

AS YOUR UNIT OF STUDY DRAWS TO A CLOSE, *you need to plan for your celebration. As always, you'll want children to look through their writing and to select their best work for this occasion. You'll want them to fix up and fancy up their writing. "Fixing up" can involve content revisions: Is this the best you can make it? Have you used precise words, written with details, reread to check that it makes sense?*

"Fixing up" will involve editing. You'll want to look over your students' work and think what lessons about conventions you could teach that might be applicable to many of them. Perhaps they could profit from you reminding them to reread to check for end punctuation. Perhaps this will be a good time to teach the conventions of punctuating dialogue.

Also, you'll want to use this occasion to remind children that spelling matters and that they need to take extra time to make it easy for people to read their writing.

In this session, you'll teach children how to make and use an editing checklist as a guide for editing.

THE MINILESSON

Connection

Remind your children that they know how to prepare for publication. Tell them you'll teach them how to check their work.

"Writers, our authors' celebration is coming up and so you'll want to reread all the writing you've done and choose the piece you want to fix up and fancy up for our celebration. When you've chosen the piece, you already know how to reread it and to ask, 'Is this my best?' You already know how to check that you've written with details and that it makes sense. What I want to teach you today is the part that you may not know. I want to show you how I check for correctness."

Teaching

Tell students that writers have Trouble Lists. These lists remind writers of things to check.

"One day, my writing teacher Don Murray told me every writer needs a Trouble List. On that list, we put the things that give us trouble. I've often had trouble spelling *happening*, so he put that on my list. For some of you, the spelling of *said* is on your Trouble List. Don made my list for me. He told me to watch out for the word *very*. 'You don't need *very*,' he told me. 'If you are very mad, you are furious. If you run very fast, you race.'"

"Then he put *nice* and *okay* on my list. He told me, 'The picnic in the park has to be something more than *okay* or *nice*. That doesn't tell me anything! Was it *peaceful*? Was it *frenetic*? Was it *steaming hot*?' He said, 'You can't say *nice* or *okay* in your writing.'"

"So this time, before we fix up our writing, every one of us needs a Trouble List. Then when we look over our writing, our list can remind us of things to check."

I begin this minilesson by recalling the way children have prepared for publication during earlier units of study. Whereas most minilessons harken back to the work of the preceding day, some instead refer to work from earlier in the year.

This is a true story. Murray also told me I used adjectives instead of precise nouns (the young dog instead of the puppy) and adverbs instead of precise verbs (walked quietly instead of tip-toed), but I don't think these chidren are ready for these bits of advice!

Active Engagement

Have students brainstorm a list of words that are vague or ordinary in their writing. Tell them that everyone has different words that they need to work on.

"I'm going to give you some paper and a clipboard and I want each of you to start making your own Trouble List," I said. Then I pointed to a list of possible items for such a list and said, "I've put some possibilities up here, on this chart paper, but these won't *all* be troublesome for all of you."

Link

Remind them to use all they know about fixing up their writing. Part of today will be to work on the Trouble List.

"Choose five things for your Trouble List, and when your list is done, you can go and get started choosing a piece to fix up for publication. Remember that you'll fix it up *every way you know how*—but part of that will be to use your Trouble List as a reminder."

TIME TO CONFER

Remember that when you help K–2 children edit their work, the goal can't be perfection. The goal instead is for each child to continually get stronger in his or her abilities to edit writing. If a child learns to use quotation marks (even if these aren't absolutely correct), it's okay that the child's writing still lacks paragraphs! The goal is that each child moves steadily forward. You'll probably want to bring small groups together and to teach strategy lessons around editing concepts that pertain to that group.

 This conference in *The Conferring Handbook* may be especially helpful today:

▶ *"Famous Writers Use Periods to Tell Readers When to Stop"*

Also, if you have *Conferring with Primary Writers,* you may want to refer to the conferences in part three.

Read aloud some student work that has improved as a result of the Trouble Lists.

"We have been working on fixing up our writing. There is always a lot to do.

Let's look at what a couple of writers changed today in their writing. Rachael changed the word *very*. She said that she was 'very sick.' Rachael changed it to, 'I was so sick that my nose wouldn't stop dripping.'"

"OOOOO! Gross!"

"Exactly! You get a better idea of how sick she was. Eric had 'and then his cat jumped into his lap.' And he changed it to 'Suddenly.' Wow, we get a better sense of how it happened. How many kids changed a *very*? I know that is a popular one! Will you share with your partner the way you used your Trouble List today? Show how you made changes in your writing. If you have a difficult time thinking about other ways to say things, ask your partner for some advice."

WRITING "ABOUT THE AUTHOR" BLURBS

GETTING READY

▶ Chart paper and markers

▶ Stack of familiar books, several for each partnership

▶ Books (one for every partnership) with "about the author" sections, for example, *Meanest Thing to Say* by Bill Cosby, *Appalachia* by Cynthia Rylant, *Owl Moon* by Jane Yolen

⊙ See CD-ROM for resources

THE BEST—THE VERY BEST—PART OF WRITING A BOOK *comes at the end when you get to choose a cover, write a dedication, fuss over the book's layout, and finally, hold the finished book in your hands.*

Children, too, deserve the fun of these final stages. They'll love designing their cover, anointing each cover with a replica of the Caldecott Award, adding call numbers onto the book's spine, and placing library cards on the back cover. This may sound like frivolity, but this "frivolity" helps me, at least, to have the energy to write. And the truth is that it isn't frivolous at all to help children dress up as writers. Life is a drama, and we each play the roles we're assigned to play. How important it is that we be sure all our children see themselves as writers.

In this session, you'll help children make a special kind of reading-writing connection. You'll ask them to study real books to notice ways authors fancy up their books for publication, and then you'll invite them to do likewise. You'll anticipate that when you ask your children to notice what published writers do to turn a draft into a real book, they'll notice "about the author" sections, dedications, copyright information, and so on. Your plan will be to suggest that your children add similar sections into their own books.

THE MINILESSON

Connection

Tell your writers that before they publish their work, they have a chance to go over it one last time to see how to make it the best it can be.

> "Writers, it's time to fancy up your books for publication. This is my favorite part of writing. I love it when my books are almost done and I just need to dress them up before I send them out into the world. So today, let's look at published books by authors we love and notice what we still need to do so our books can be published."

Teaching and Active Engagement

Pass out a stack of familiar books and ask the children to study them, looking for finishing touches for their own books.

> "I'm going to pass out a bunch of books, books you know well. Will you and your partner look over the book you've given and ask, 'How did this writer fancy up his or her book for publication?' If you notice something the writer did, put a sticky note on that page. Later we'll compare notes and make a big list."
> Soon the children were poring over books, marking noteworthy sections.

Children love these open-ended invitations to pore over literature, noticing what other authors have done.

After a time, gather children and collect a list of what they've noticed. Suggest children may also want to write "about the author" sections.

> "So let's compile what we noticed."
> - Get a cover
> - Put author's name and title on the cover
> - Write a dedication
> - Write an author blurb

> "In this unit, we've often noticed what an author has done and then tried the same thing in our own writing. I'm wondering, would any of you be willing to make a cover for your writing and to put your name on it as the author? Thumbs up. Great. Would any of you be willing to dedicate your book to

Of course you know children will definitely be excited to make a cover!

someone and to write, 'Dedicated to _____' (and maybe a sentence or two) inside the front cover? Wonderful. What about writing an 'about the author' section?" The kids looked uncertain.

Pass out a book with an "about the author" section for each partnership. Tell children to read them over.

"I have brought a team of special teachers who can teach us how to write 'about the author' blurbs," I motioned towards a pile of books. "Are you willing to work with special teachers?" The class nodded yes.

"Fantastic!" I doled out the books. "A teacher for you, and a teacher for you. So class, we're going to have a little bit longer minilesson than usual today. Would you and your partner stay right here and take lessons from your teacher about what goes into the 'about the author' sections?"

Help the children process what an "about the author" section contains.

After a few minutes, I reconvened the class, "What sorts of things do authors usually tell about in their 'about the author' sections? Who can read us your 'about the author' blurb?"

Joe read the "about the author" blurb from Cosby's *Meanest Thing to Say* and the class agreed on three items Cosby included. Children read the blurb from *Owl Moon* and *Appalachia* by Cynthia Rylant and added more items to the list.

If your children can't read these yet, you'll need to alter this section of the minilesson so that you read these sections aloud.

You will want to select books for children to study with some care.

Link

Remind children to take what they've learned today and use it to get their own books ready to publish.

"So class, we have a lot of work to do and not a lot of time. You'll want to spend today's workshop fancying up your book and you can decide how. You might finish making sure your spelling and your punctuation are as perfect as they can be. You might add a dedication, or anything else you see when you study your books. Some of you will want to have 'about the author' sections. All of our drafts need to be ready to go to the publishing house by lunchtime because during lunch and this afternoon, some of your moms and dads will be here helping us to print your books. Thumbs up when you know what you're going to do." As children signaled, I waved them to get started.

WHAT MIGHT GO INTO AN "ABOUT THE AUTHOR" BLURB

* What the author is known for
* Other books the author has written
* Where the author went to school
* Why the author selected this subject to write about
* What this book means to the author

Remember that minilessons add to children's repertoire of options. You don't need to insist that each child write an about the author blurb.

TIME TO CONFER

Today you'll probably want to encourage children to articulate what they've learned.

For children who are still editing, you may want to revisit and revise minilessons from earlier units of study that help writers to be readers of their writing. See *Revision*, Session V or *Small Moments*, Session XI.

You may want to point out that a single book can teach writers lots of lessons. Children can learn word choice, sight words, punctuation, and spelling from any book. They can learn about characters and settings, leads and endings, showing-not-telling, and detail and dialogue from almost any story. Invite children to mine even just one page of one book for zillions of possible lessons, not just how to write an About the Author blurb.

These conferences in *The Conferring Handbook* may be especially helpful today:

▶ *"You Can Use Ellipses to Show Waiting"*

▶ *"Use a Refrain"*

▶ *"I See You're Adding an Exclamation Mark to Your Story Like Mem Fox Does"*

Also, if you have *Conferring with Primary Writers*, you may want to refer to the conferences in part five.

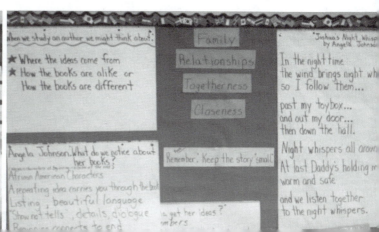

TALKING AND READING TO AN AUDIENCE: AN AUTHOR'S CELEBRATION

GETTING READY

- Chart with students' names in groups of three and a designated area in which to sit
- Teacher's finished piece
- Author study baskets
- "Craft" chart
- Overhead projector and transparencies of *Joshua's Night Whispers*
- "About the author" scripts for MCs on clipboards, organized by groups of three
- Students' best works
- See CD-ROM for resources

YOUR CHILDREN HAVE NOW SPENT FIVE MONTHS LEARNING THE CRAFT *of strong narrative writing, and their work is a testimony to all they've learned. Next month, you and your children will embark on new terrain. This will be exciting, but it won't yield gorgeous texts like those you have before you now. So, this is a good time to invite the whole world in to see and to celebrate.*

Author celebrations are political. By showcasing good work, author celebrations also showcase the literacy standards and beliefs of a classroom and a school. They remind everyone present that any discussion of standards, assessment, or curriculum is really a discussion about real children and their teachers. Invite the superintendent, members of the board of education, the school's PTA president, and the reporters. This will be more stress than you need in your life, but you stand a chance of changing the course of education in your school. Budgets, programs, and staffing decisions for the year ahead are usually made in the next few months. How important it is for policy makers to enter those negotiations remembering your children and the lump in the throat they had as they listened to them!

This celebration should reveal the work of this unit in all its glory. You'll want your children to show the guests the astute, close observations they've learned to make about the texts they read. This will be most evident if you ask your guests to read Joshua's Night Whispers *and to think, "What has Angela Johnson done that I can admire and learn from?" and then you let your guests listen in on your children addressing that same question. Or, have a few selected children speak or read to the crowd, each elaborating on another point that they notice in the text and perhaps each also reading their writing to show how they did likewise in their own writing.*

The Celebration

Read aloud *Joshua's Night Whispers,* and give visitors a few minutes to discuss it. Then read it to them again, this time letting the children share their thoughts with the audience.

"Guests, may I interrupt? I'm going to reread *Joshua's Night Whispers* and this time, will the children talk to each other about what they notice Angela doing? They will talk also about why she might have done this." Again, Amanda read the text and this time, children talked afterwards. Since there was time after the children had each mentioned one thing, they each took another turn, talking about a second observation.

Tell the audience you've all studied Angela Johnson to inform your own writing. Tell them the procedure for listening to the children's writing.

"Guests and writers, may I stop you? We studied Angela Johnson and other authors for one big reason. We wanted them to become our teachers, and we wanted to learn things that would make our writing better. So now, let's listen to the writing *we* did."

"Three writers will share their writing with all of us, and you can watch the way we do it. Then, in each of your groups, the three writers will do the same thing. Each group needs to have one guest, not a writer, who'll be the Master of Ceremonies, the MC. I'll be that for these three writers, but before I go further, may I have a volunteer MC from each group?" When someone volunteered, Amanda gave that person a clipboard that held a script.

Demonstrate the procedure for listening and commenting by having three writers read to everyone, interspersed with comments.

"I'll be the MC for this group. What will happen is I (or your MC) will read aloud an introduction for each author. Then the author will read his or her story. Then we'll tell the author something he or she has done that we admire and might learn from (just two things). Then the MC will introduce the next author. Let's get started."

The only risk was that the children would all be so anxious to impress that they'd talk at once, on top of each other, so we'd planned a sequence for who'd talk first, second, third. Each child had also chosen two things to discuss and had resolved to say as much as possible about each thing. They tended to discuss that this book wasn't a list of things but was instead a focused small moment, the presence of ellipses, the comeback phrase, the detail, the lists, the word choice as in "night whispers" not "sounds," the fact that Joshua changes, and much more.

One way to make this read-aloud work is by projecting overhead transparencies of the pages (with the permission of the publisher) on a large screen in an auditorium.

"Parents, grandparents, other caretakers, school leaders, and writers, we've gathered here to celebrate an extraordinary group of young writers. I'd like to introduce one of them."

"Justin Selig is famous in our class for being the first to try ellipses . . . and a lot of other things. He is enthusiastic about all things, bringing jazz-band like energy to our classroom." Justin read *The Jazz Music* aloud, while Amanda showed it on the overhead projector. Then a few people said what they admired about his writing.

"It's good how you tell what happened first and next and next . . . First you were walking to the auditorium and you heard the music, then you were dancing."

"You really show that you like jazz music."

"You don't just say, 'The end!' You show your feelings at the end."

Soon I'd introduced the next two readers, each time reading a blurb I'd written about them, and for each, the audience responded with detailed feedback.

"Lindsay is so good at making long stories out of small moments that she can write a whole book about the excitement of waiting for the elevator, carrying her friend, to arrive on her floor!" [*Fig. XVII-1*]

"Sergio is a real author. He knows the magic for turning words into stories, and for turning a tree into a ship, a gas station, a fort. His imagination keeps all of us seeing miracles in the little moments."

Tell the groups in the audience to copy the procedure you just went through in their own groups.

"Now in your small group, the MC will play my role. You'll introduce the writer and help draw out two—just two—detailed responses, then move to the next writer."

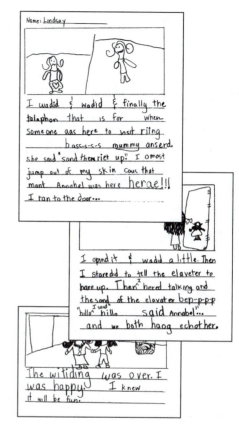

Fig. XVII-1 Lindsay